The Organization Trap

THE
ORGANIZATION
TRAP

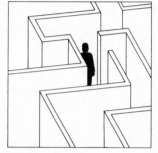

AND
HOW
TO GET OUT OF IT

SAMUEL A. CULBERT

Basic Books, Inc., Publishers

NEW YORK

Library of Congress Catalog Card Number: 74–79281
SBN: 465–05320–3
Printed in the United States of America
DESIGNED BY VINCENT TORRE
74 75 76 77 78   10 9 8 7 6 5 4 3 2 1

Brindis:

por el público y para el público

CONTENTS

ACKNOWLEDGMENTS

After a number of false starts I wound up writing the kind of book I wanted to write, but couldn't when I began. I did it with the help of the best people imaginable. They taught me, challenged me, and empathized with me. Their support helped me maintain focus during the long days I worked alone.

From the beginning I wanted to write an engaging book about the mantraps in organization life. I wanted to communicate my message to a diverse audience. But I learned to write in the academic system, and that doesn't always make for interesting reading. Mort Lachman was convinced that if I put enough of myself into my writing I could give my book the appeal I wanted it to have. He spent many hours reading my manuscript and encouraging me to loosen it up. He stuck with me from false start to false start, from start to finish. Mort is the most interesting writer I know, and he turned out to be an exceptional teacher.

Next I needed someone to read what I wrote and question me on organization and clarity. Susan Nero did this and more. Her judgment, creativity, and good taste greatly enhanced the quality of what I wrote. Susan has a special way of being direct with criticism that left my ego intact. She was generous with her time and nurturing. In fact I can't imagine anyone being so generous with me again.

Then I needed a sharp professional mind to scrutinize what I was saying and put it to the test of his own experience and logic. My close friend and UCLA colleague Bob Tannenbaum filled this role perfectly. He didn't miss a thing. Of course we saw many things differently, and this meant some penetrating and emotional discussions. Bob doesn't shrink from conflict; yet he's known as one of the kindest men in the fields of humanistic and organizational psychology. While there are a number of differences we didn't resolve, I'd be surprised if there's one we didn't discuss.

A number of friends really came through when I needed them. They critiqued preliminary drafts of my manuscript and helped me negotiate its publication. Their enthusiasm and willingness to help meant a great deal. They are Dick Kirshberg, Warren Bennis, Stan Hinckley, Chris Argyris, and Matt Miles.

There were a number of people who were particularly good listeners and challengers during the period when I was formulating my ideas and putting them into order. Many of my ideas were half-baked, and they saw to it that I didn't go too long without recognizing the soft spots. In particular I remember an elementary question on a Cape Cod beach that provoked a two-hour headache. The people involved include Bill McKelvey, Dick Laskey, Oscar Ortsman, Bo Ohlström, Max Elden, Jack McDonough, Dick Walton, Dick Snyder, Ray Lademann, Don Yates, Ralph Merritt, Harry Dunlop, Larry Lodico, Russ Parks, and Allen Koplin.

Then there were people who were in support groups with me during the time I was writing this book. They offered me companionship when the going was tough and helped me grapple with the problems I was writing about that also touched me personally. These people include some of the above plus Kouji Nakata, Roy Gregg, Tuck Taylor, Frank Jackson, Harry Walker, Will McWhinney, and Warren Schmidt.

My wife, JoAnn, and I had a semiserious joke during one period of my writing. We said I should dedicate the book to her, "Without whose help I would have finished six months earlier." In the end, however, she pitched in and enhanced my thinking with her love and critique.

Our first child, Samantha, was born shortly after I began my book. I spent much of my writing time at home, which turned out to be an unexpected chance to watch her become a very big little kid. During periods of abstract thinking and intellectualism she provided a reliable connection to my loving and tender feelings.

Who would ever think that a small book like this could productively utilize an army of secretaries and typists? Here too I was exceptionally fortunate. While I didn't have an army, not even a platoon, I had a marvelous person on whom I could always count, Pat Riley, and others, Eileen Yamada, Sophia Behrstock, and Carol Graszler, who graciously pitched in when we needed help. I also received assistance in the form of a small grant from the Human Systems Development research center of the Graduate School of Management at UCLA.

Last I want to thank Martin Kessler, the Editorial Director of Basic Books. His taste and his confidence in me added considerably to the book you're about to read.

PART I

The Traps of Organization Life

CHAPTER 1

We've Lost Control
and Hardly Know It

The Problem

The other day I heard a speech given by the outgoing deputy director of a medium-sized public organization. As he stepped forward to speak, tears began streaming down his face. To the audience's surprise, he did not try to cover up. There were no platitudes about his sorrow in leaving. Instead, he frankly admitted his tears were of pain and disappointment for allowing himself to be chewed up by the system. He told how during his tenure he had seen this happen to others, but had never thought it could happen to him. He even went so far as to claim the system ruined him.

What did this man mean when he said he was chewed up by the system? His speech, actually an assortment of semicoherent phrases, told his story. He had compromised himself and now felt he had achieved little. He saw himself falling into established ways of doing things, even when he sensed they were outmoded. He knew change was needed, but he never could quite come up with practical alternatives. He could not stop battling with immediate issues long enough to grope with inadequacies he perceived in the way the organization was being run. After a while, he noticed that when someone else raised a problem he would automatically switch the topic and explain how things were better than they used to be. Yet he couldn't completely dismiss his feeling that things weren't right. In the end, he failed to take stands equal to his insights about what needed to be changed and only half-heartedly supported the system. He recognized that in other peoples' minds he was neither a well-intentioned visionary nor a decisive leader. And worst of all, he said, he agreed with them, although he was sure he couldn't have done a better job.

The dilemmas that seemed to get the best of this man are the ones that face all of us who work in large organizations. We know we can't succeed in ways that are meaningful to us merely by following organization precedent. Yet we don't know how to take stands that reflect our feelings that something needs to be changed. We can't quite specify what needs to be changed or how it can be accomplished practically.

These dilemmas are with us almost every day of our organization life. In moments of candor, we ask ourselves:

- If I spoke my mind, could I still get good grades in the organization?
- To what extent are my needs to fit in governing my actions?
- Is the organization's influence on me so subtle that I'm not aware of it?
- How extreme will the compromises I'm making have to get before I'm forced to sit down and take stock of myself?
- Even if I face up to my compromises, would I be able to do anything about them?
- Am I so conditioned to seeing things the accepted way that I've lost my sense of objectivity?
- Have I gone too far in rationalizing my choices, or do I really want what I'm working for?

These questions all reflect self-doubts about the extent to which we're in control of our organization life. They are the result of knowing we've learned more from our experience than we've been able to put into words. We are often unsure of why we're doing what we are, whether or not what we're doing is in our best interests, or what alternatives are available to us. We don't tell it as we see it, and we seldom engage in friendly dialogue with others who, we've determined, see it differently.

From the day we walk into a large organization to the day we leave, we are subjected to forces that shape our picture of organization life and our beliefs about what constitutes success in it. We are subjected to an intensive socialization process; yet we have only a minimal awareness of the ways in which we're being transformed. The longer we're in the organization, the less we're aware of our indoctrination.

Only after those who are responsible for us believe that we see things a certain way do they leave us alone to act independently. Once our boss is confident that we want to be seen as worthy and will work hard to be promoted, how much control over our activities does he need to exert? If we get out of line, he can always make a midorbit correction by suggesting that it's in our best interests to do this or that. And, of course, the most difficult part of it is that our boss is unaware of how he's controlling us. From his point of view, he's merely giving us positive direction. It's this way in 99 percent of large organizations.

However, it's far too simple to say that "they're doing it to us." We're also doing it to others. In fact, as much as anybody, we're doing it to ourselves. We are the system. It's our internalization of norms, myths, beliefs, and values that perpetuates established images and implicitly censors new ways of seeing things. We make points by being what we think the organization wants us to be and so affirm the status quo. In our organization roles, we influence the direction of other people's lives and then sell *them* on what meaning their experiences holds for them.

We've created an organization world in which the system defines the man rather than one in which the nature of man determines the system. In the process, we've adapted to the point where we've lost grasp of our identity independent of the system. In trying to get others to adapt, we identify with our adaptations and our roles. What little freedom we have left to form our own identity we use to bring us closer to other people's images of who we should be.

There's a jujitsu quality to the brand of freedom we've worked out for ourselves. The momentum generated by our actions is used against us. In the process of trying to express more of our identity, we wind up expressing less. For instance, each of us has a lingering idea that he can meet the requirements of the system and still have enough time left to accomplish projects he believes in. Perhaps this is possible, but for most of us it's possible only by working fifty to seventy hours a week on a job successful people are supposed to handle in forty. And it doesn't occur to us that something is off when the harder we work for certain benefits, the more we grow to prize these benefits; the more we actually accumulate, the harder we work to accumulate more. We wind up seeking freedom from external controls in ways that all but guarantee that such freedom will elude us.

In effect, we've lost control of our organization life. The images that determine what we want and how we act to get it are too often externally imposed. Moreover, we're not using the information available in our experience which could tell us when we're allowing ourselves to be directed by the system and what we need to know to formulate alternatives that reflect our real self-interests.

We and the organization both have plenty to gain by our developing greater control over our organization lives. We could avoid ulcers, heart attacks, depressions, and nervous breakdowns, and the organization could count on having access to our most vital forms of participation. We could form adventurous, trusting, and intimate relationships with work associates, and the organization would benefit from nondefensive, creative, and direct communications. We could balk at performing meaningless tasks merely because they provide visible evidence of our productivity, and the organization would get the messages needed to reexamine and upgrade its goals. We could expose our weaknesses, self-doubts, and vulnerabilities to those who might help and support us, and the organization could count on our not becoming obsolete. We could spend more time trying to help others rather than trying to control them, and the organization could avoid the inefficiency of power struggles and political scheming. We could escape the provincialism of our own limited perspectives, and the organization could enjoy the benefits of people collaborating and building on one another's ideas. The possibilities are endless.

The Approach

This book contains an approach designed to show you how to exert greater control over your organization life. Part I describes the man-traps in organization life, traps that lead us to believe we're in control of our lives when we're not. Part II provides the understanding we need to recognize what makes us fall into these traps. It also gives us the theory we need for working our way out. Part III contains a strategy for actually freeing ourselves from the traps. It teaches us how to formulate alternatives to the organization life we now lead.

As much as any single factor, it is our inability to formulate alternatives to current procedures that keeps us from gaining control of our organization life. As long as we're dependent on the perspectives and suggestions of others, we will continue to lack control over our life in the organization. Consequently, this book is directed toward helping us develop our own perspectives. It will help us assess what's actually going on in our work world, what's in our own best interests, and what kind of relationship we've formed with the organization for which we work. Then we should be able to envision alternatives that provide a better match between our interests and those of the organization.

CHAPTER 2

The Subjective Nature of Organization Life

Let's face it. We work for our organization because we think it's good for us. We've scanned the alternatives, and for now this one seems the best we can do. If some other organization better met our needs, we'd quit our present jobs and go to work for it. If our needs changed, we'd start thinking about other places to work. If many of us found our needs changing, and the organization wanted us to stay around, the organization would have to change its system. It changed for minorities when they asserted their identities, it has begun changing for women, and it will change again when we're able to understand and express our own interests.

This book is written about life in white-collar America today and the actions we can take to change it. The book comes from what I've witnessed, both as a participant and as a consultant, in large industrial corporations, state and federal agencies, school systems, universities, city governments, mental health agencies, religious organizations, and organizations doing community development work in the United States and abroad. The concepts I write about apply to each organization level, from first-level staff to their managers, and up the hierarchy to the top.

Because organization life in America is dominated by men, this book focuses on. I think these concepts apply to women as well, but it's men whom I've seen chewed up by the system. They are the ones who act as if they were in control of their organization life while they are being blown about by forces they cannot identify.

7

Throughout this book I use the term "organization system" to reference the variety of externals with which we concern ourselves when we start thinking about how our actions will be received. These externals include concerns for both the specific organization for which we work and the social, economic, and political systems that characterize the American work culture. But whether we use the term organization system or some comparable one, what we're talking about is not necessarily what exists. As often as not, what we think of as external and as a reaction to our efforts is a product of our own subjectivity. Whether we're concerned about a demanding boss, a dependent work group, an inaccessible upper management, an extremely conservative code of professional ethics, or a tight job market, what we see is not necessarily what's out there.

While we can get better at specifying what's out there, it's not something we're likely to be very precise in describing. We're not able to experience directly with our five senses such things as a promotion system, a managerial philosophy, or a corporate ethic. However, we can attain more objectivity through experimentation. We can take seriously people who see things differently, struggle to identify our biases, try out new approaches, and investigate exceptions to the rule. To deny that we can learn more inevitably sentences us to insularity and less control of our organization life.

The closer we come to discovering what's out there, the more likely we are to discover that it has far less coherence than we've been attributing to it. We cope with the randomness that actually characterizes the organization world by making patterns out of events, perceptions, and feelings that have no natural relationship with one another. But we think of these patterns as if they constituted an organization system because we need a way of orienting ourselves.

Using a concept like the organization system gives us a way of talking with others about the impact and value of our work. It's a shorthand way of pulling together the intangibles of organization life. It allows us to talk about the goals, the ways we're supposed to operate, and the constraints which we believe must be observed. However, what we're talking about is quite subjective, and each person has something different in mind. Yet the words we use are sufficiently broad and abstract that others can respond as if they know exactly to what we're referring. When we're talking to close associates and hit upon differences in what we think the organization world is, we usually are more than willing to compromise and reach an easy agreement. But the farther we get from our work unit, our profession, or the organization for which we work, the less likely we are to compromise and find an easy resolution to our differences.

Part of what we attribute to the organization system is made up of the rules, norms, and values that characterize the organization for which we work, even though many of these are not found in the procedures manual. We start learning about them the day we are interviewed for our job and continue learning about them until the day we leave. Some of the things we learn are unique to our organization, but many are behaviors and attitudes that are required in any organization. The more organizations we work for, the less we have to learn. However, within our own organization, we get crash courses when we are new in the organization and in training, when we change jobs, get promoted, join a new work unit, or deviate grossly from what's expected of us.

Part of what we attribute to the organization system is learned by experience in the social, economic, and political spheres of our society. This learning includes the assumptions we make about the value and usefulness of people, the marketing and production needs of the economy, and the competitive and political processes of organizations and government. It encompasses our expectations of what people in different roles ought to do and how they ought to behave. And, more generally, it includes our beliefs about the purpose of work and the ethical and moral values which ought to be observed, as well as the conditions under which it's permissible to deviate from them. We start learning about the system when we're children and become aware of organizations, the different roles people assume in them, and the privileges that go along with ascending the hierarchy. We get crash courses when attending professional school, when under financial pressure, when our personal security is rocked, and when social crises such as racism, pollution, censorship, or inflation affect us.

As we've come to know it, the organization system is often an *in*human one. While we are part of it, many of the assumptions we make about ourselves deviate from our inherent qualities and our innate capacities. We tailor ourselves to meet the production needs of the organization and to fit within some arbitrarily drawn organization chart. If we are salesmen, we think we should be aggressive, if managers, we think we should be patient and analytic, and if scientists, we think we should work independently. The image of man to which we conform is the result of generations of people adapting to social struc-

9

tures which are valued for their practicality; yet we use these social structures to determine our ideals.

Through generations of adapting to the existing organization system, we have been cut off from the natural human qualities that characterize us more accurately. We are sufficiently removed from knowing and expressing these qualities that we can't discover them with a single insight. Rather we must move in progressively. We can avail ourselves of new insights, modify our behavior accordingly, and expect that living an organization life that more closely approximates our potential will provide us with additional insights and further possibilities. There's more than one way for people to organize in forming a profitable and socially responsible organization, and we have the opportunity to discover a way that better allows us to be our uncompromised selves.

Organizing in such a way will give us the control we're looking for. Creating that system depends on raising our consciousness by learning who we are without our adaptations to the organization system, what the system is and how it operates (contrasted with what others in the organization lead us to believe), and what assumptions underlie our relationship with the system.

We would have developed these perspectives before, but we lacked the skills to learn from our experiences and mistrusted the validity of what we did learn. Thus, I see consciousness as the essence of gaining more control, and consciousness-raising as the process leading toward an organization life which better approximates our humanity. The consciousness I deal with in this book is rational. It is based on the belief that what we learn will lend itself to a new order that will proceed with continuity from where we are. However, I believe even more control is available as we learn emotional and spiritual lessons as well.

Gaining control is not a matter of absolutes. Consciousness is a slowly expanding commodity, and the increased control that follows takes place gradually. One does not seize control, one develops control. As long as we're having new experiences, there is more for us to learn and integrate.

Learning the lessons of our experience means accepting insights that go counter to the prevailing organization culture. This can be a disorienting and lonely task when attempted individually. For this reason, and others that will be discussed, the consciousness-raising approach described in this book is accomplished in a group. People with like problems, faced with similar constraints, can do much to support one another. Moreover, a group can be far more objective and thorough than a single person. In a sense, a group of people supporting one another forms a counterculture that buffers members against the prevailing culture's pressure to conform.

However, I don't think this type of counterculture is likely to seek the destruction of the organization system as we know it. It will instead help us around our cultural bias of preferring the undesirable known to the feared unknown. Before we make a fatal change, we'll have time to assess it. If we go too far, we'll find out, back up a step, and search for new alternatives.

Each new insight and perspective paves the way for learning things that were not possible to realize at a previous stage of consciousness. For this reason, I *don't* make substantive proposals that state exactly what we ought to be striving for. Instead, I propose a consciousness-raising method that helps us learn from our experience and evolve organization lives that fit us better than the ones we're currently living.

Advocating a specific method that people ought to follow in order to gain more control involves a contradiction. If people can't gain control spontaneously and individually, then aren't we merely replacing one cage with another? On one hand, we have to get rid of any structure that narrows our focus in order to gain control. On the other hand, we need some structure to comprehend the limits of whatever method we're using to accomplish our goals. Although the contradiction remains, I believe the approach used in this book increases our capacity to recognize the structural limits as they exist and are created.

The approach used in this book is a positive one even though it begins by pointing out what's wrong with the organization system and what's wrong with us before we even enter the system. I begin this way because our energy for improving the ways organizations work and the ways we relate to them comes from our seeing what's wrong. We can no longer afford to treat organizations as if they were divine. Ultimately, we must treat them as what they are—artificial and arbitrarily created entities invented by humans. Today we have the capacity to improve vastly the quality of our organization life. The time has come for us to reconsider the basics of how we organize to do work.

CHAPTER 3

Mantraps in How the Organization Operates

> . . . A trap is a trap only for a creature which cannot solve the problems that it sets. Man-traps are dangerous only in relation to the limitations on what men can see and value and do. The nature of the trap is a function of the nature of the trapped. To describe either is to imply the other.
>
> Geoffrey Vickers

What we've come to know as the organization system sets mantraps for us. These traps take the form of assumptions about how the organization system operates. We assume that what others imply is happening is in fact happening. These traps go unnoticed because of our willingness to compromise our own identity in order to be accepted within the system. And these traps secure our compromise. They prevent us from recognizing when we're out of control and from understanding what we have to do to gain control.

The assumptions that form these traps are not so much incorrect as they are incomplete. Without more complete perspectives we stay trapped. Gaining more control begins by explicating these assumptions and questioning how they might be incomplete or even inaccurate.

The following is a sampling of assumptions commonly made by those of us who work for large organizations. They indicate some areas where we are out of control of our organization life. Reading about them gives an indication of what we're up against. However, the type of understanding we actually need to exercise greater control will come only after we've identified mantraps as they are uniquely present in our *own* organization life.

Assumptions That Are Mantraps

• *When the organization offers us choices, alternatives, and latitude in personal actions, we assume that we are actually gaining control over our organization life.* We grasp at every choice, opportunity, and latitude in action as if it constituted real control. We believe we have control even though the choices we're selecting from were established for us by others. At the same time, we blind ourselves to the choices we are *not* allowed to make, including many of the career and life issues which are of fundamental importance to us. For instance, we believe we're in control when we're left on our own to decide such details as when to travel and whether or not to go first class at the company's expense. But we neglect to question the real issues involved, like whether we must travel or why long-distance traveling always seems to be done on weekends.

Perhaps our biggest illusion about being in control takes place when, as frequently happens, we are offered a personal option but without the information we need to reach an independent decision. If we were really in control, we'd demand the information on the grounds that it's *our* organization life. Instead, we ask advice of someone, such as our boss, who should know what's best for us. Or we decide blindly, making the wrong decision or the right decision for the wrong reasons. In any case, we leave to chance a decision that really needs careful consideration.

Recently, I sat in on a management problem-solving meeting and had an opportunity to see how an illusion of choice gets played out. A salesman named Hugo was under discussion. The issue involved was subtle, which of course is what makes it a mantrap.

Hugo could never have suspected he had created a problem large enough to be debated by his division's top team. He was considered such a good salesman that his boss wanted to keep him with the division even though the decision had been made to discontinue selling their product line in his territory. But Hugo didn't want to move from the Los Angeles area.

His boss presented the issue this way. "We found a job for Hugo in the East, but I don't know whether we can get him to take it. We'll have to let someone else go to make room for him, but if Hugo will move, it'll be worth it. I'm anticipating Hugo will give us some trouble. It seems his family very much wants to stay in L.A. The kids don't want to change schools, the wife has a sick mother in the area, and they like their house. I've called around to see who might pick him up. It would be a shame to let a good man like this slip out of the company. I called the X division and finally convinced them I wasn't trying to peddle off a dud. They'd be glad to have him work in Denver. I also called the Y division from where we got Hugo, and they'd be glad to let him have his old job back in West Los Angeles. My plan is to offer Hugo our job in the East and hold back the other options. I want to entice him as much as I can. Then if he turns *us* down, we can mention the other options."

Despite the boss's presentation I got the impression that he actually likes Hugo. I think he was phrasing his dilemma in the proper terms hoping that the other managers would encourage him to tell Hugo all the options in the first place. But they didn't. I doubt if it would have been any consolation to Hugo to learn that the uppermost management also thinks about *these* men the same way that they were thinking about him. Regardless of how far Hugo may have gotten in the decision-tree, how much choice did he really get?!

• *When the organization says we have control of a job, we assume that we do in fact have control of the job.* In contrast to the old days when a manager would tell us exactly how he thought a job ought to be done, today's supervisory technique gives us a wide-open field and words of confidence in our ability to do a good job. The manager's role is to "underdefine" what needs to be done, which has the effect of making us come back regularly for his critique. It is by critiquing what we've already done that our manager exposes us to the ideas and standards that he had in mind in the first place, but couldn't state for fear of shutting off our creativity. Realistically, of course, he's less concerned over losing our creativity than over reducing his authority over us. This can have the effect of putting us on the firing line in high-risk situations without sufficient understanding to perform adequately. No wonder so many of us eventually refuse offers of increased autonomy, even when it's the real thing.

Recently, I asked a middle manager I know fairly well if he'd ever had such an experience. "All the time," he replied angrily. He went on to add some nuances. "By the time my boss critiques a project I've been working on, I feel totally responsible for all the things that can go wrong and no longer can even take credit for the positive outcomes. As a result, I feel inadequate as hell and stupid for once again buying the assumption that I could have done the job alone in the first place. How many times I've gotten the call from a boss that 'Mr. Big would like to hear what's going on in your area.' I always ask, 'What does Mr. Big want to hear?' and I always get back, 'He merely wants to get caught up.' I think to myself, it's a performance, and I better be good because I don't get to see Mr. Big that often. I spend days preparing, and I get my men to help, which means passing the same broad question down the line. And after anywhere from a couple of days to two weeks of preparation, I wind up being given twenty minutes to say what I know." He then added, "The thing that really grinds me is that if you asked me to address the local PTA and wouldn't tell me what they wanted to hear, I'd tell you to shove it, and here I obediently march off to do what I'm asked."

Having control of one's job can be a mixed blessing. Defining a job or problem so broadly that there is no one perfect answer ultimately makes us turn to higher-ups for project definition. While this manager was given the freedom to do whatever he wanted, he lacked the control to get others to declare their expectations of him. Only then could he have had the choice to go along with their request or argue for a more relevant orientation.

• *When the organization implies that we will have greater control over our organization life as we climb the organization ladder, we assume that we will in fact gain control.* There's a terrible irony to this assumption. What we have to do to be promoted by the organization system often destroys our ability to think in terms that allow us to exercise control. Even though we can order others around, it does not follow that we can control our own lives. Too often our buying into the system is done at the expense of buying out of our uniqueness. I'm reminded of the conformity that takes place in a large Hollywood talent agency. Every talent agent wears a black suit, a white-on-white shirt, and a thin dark tie. And everyone is short. As legend has it, one day a tall guy went to work there, and the next day he was short.

For people at the bottom and middle levels, success is measured by promotion. To be promoted, we have to demonstrate our loyalty to the organization, and we assume that the best way to do this is to make self-sacrificing decisions. The mantrap involved in this assumption is apparent to me whenever I see people repeatedly demonstrate their loyalty to the organization with self-sacrificing decisions, each time without realizing it. We fail to learn that organizations have short

15

memories for past sacrifices, except in the most heroic instances. Rather, the system works to pin us down so that each situation becomes a fresh opportunity to demonstrate our loyalty.

In my consulting practice, different people approach me and relate, not without enjoyment, the worst stories of sacrifice and deprivation. Then they sheepishly look to me for appreciation. I empathized with them until it dawned on me that I was part of the collusion that kept the pattern going. My expressions of empathy and respect were being used to refuel them to go back and do more of the same.

Some might reason that the system is built on such sacrifice and would crumble if people stopped giving their pound of flesh. Well, if that's the case, I say it's time to look for alternatives. While discussing this point, a manager once turned to me and asked rhetorically, "What use does society have for people?"

It's not that I'm against sacrifice or pain as a consequence of doing what's good for the organization when we don't know a better way. I do it myself, and I do it because I value the organization and its ability to provide products for society and benefits for me that are greater than what we can accomplish by ourselves. But self-sacrificing heroics are not necessarily good for the organization. They lead to short-term solutions and provide only temporary relief from failures in the way the organization works which, if not faced up to now, will come back to haunt us another day.

We might think that our reasons for sacrifice spring from our own needs to get ahead, not just from the organization's. The fallacy in this reasoning is demonstrated each time someone who supposedly has made it, brags about the power, possessions, status, or rewards he's already achieved, but is dreaming of more of what he already has. Typically, that person underestimates the range of his potential for self-expression and competence. For example, while almost every member of top management complains about the loneliness and isolation of his job, it's hard to get even one to think about a colleague group with whom he could share his knotty questions, gain philosophical perspectives, or just have fun. One would think this would be the sort of environment a person truly in control of his job would create for himself.

• *When the organization says its effectiveness depends on holding us accountable for whatever we do or fail to do, we assume that it can in fact hold us accountable.* If we didn't assume that we were in control of our organization life, we would instantly see the mantrap embedded in this assumption. Much of our organization life involves going along with precedents, without a good perspective of what we're doing or why we're doing it a certain way. Yet when something goes wrong, we're expected to come forward and take the blame. We accept this reasoning despite the fact that most of us, most of the time, are trying to do a good job in the face of formidable odds.

It is because we lack self-confidence that we're so willing to take the blame for something we never understood in the first place, and our willingness is neither in our nor the organization's interests. If we learn anything, we merely learn which situations to avoid or how to spread the blame. We don't learn how to shake loose from precedent and take command.

This was precisely the trap that an office administrator fell into after she was hired to coordinate the work efforts of a number of senior managers. The senior managers had never agreed to have their projects overlap. But the administrator was in the dark about this and worked for six months trying to set up a system which none of the managers saw as meeting their needs. The administrator felt terrible about her lack of accomplishment, and the managers viewed her work as unsatisfactory. It wasn't until her feelings of inadequacy compelled her to quit that a meeting was called which eventually clarified the managers' nonagreement.

How we react when something goes wrong demonstrates how we're hooked by our sense of responsibility. We hear: "Why didn't you . . . ?" or "What made you think that . . . ?" We reflect: "I never thought of that," or "I'll never do that again." Our impulse is to admit our guilt and quickly get past the situation. We do penance by feeling depressed or inadequate for a sufficient period of time to absolve us of our failure, and vow to do better the next time.

But can't our responsibility extend to figuring out why we did what we did, or why we failed to do what we didn't do? Don't we have a responsibility to ourselves to reflect analytically on the problems we got into and to gain the perspective we lacked that caused us difficulty?

• *We assume that the organization is evaluating only our performance on the job and not our value as human beings.* This assumption is a real setup because it's difficult for us to view criticism of our work objectively. Our self-esteem is very fragile, and our egos are easily hurt. We personalize and internalize almost everything said to us. Someone criticizes the clarity of our report writing, and inside we react as if they were talking about our souls.

The belief that our feelings of self-worth are independent from how our work in the organization is evaluated gives management what it needs to play it both ways, however unwittingly it does so. Even on the least important issues, we feel the threat of damaged self-esteem if we don't succeed. If we fail and the hurt gets too deep, management is off the hook, because everybody knows "nothing could be all that important."

We can be so hurt that we lack the bounce to do a thoughtful job and can no longer provide ourselves with the ego boosts we need to feel vital. This hurt can build up over time so that people will undergo permanent personality changes to protect themselves. Almost anyone who has worked a few years in an organization can tell a story of how he was forced to shut down a side of himself that he prized.

Defenses can be evoked to the point where someone is accused of having retired on the job. This usually means that they have switched to a low-risk posture to avoid failure. It involves internalizing the conservative aspects of the organization system and using them to justify mediocre performance and not overstepping one's roles. It protects a person from getting into a position where he must believe the criticisms others levy at him. To some extent, this strategy succeeds. While others may view his behavior as mediocre or inadequate, his deficiencies are sufficiently predictable that it becomes other people's mistakes for expecting more from him than he can deliver. I once heard a retiree reflect, "I've given this company twenty-five of the *best* years of my life; now it's time to give it some of the other ones."

As if our problems weren't big enough, we compound them by allowing others to evaluate us any way they see fit. No matter what our organization rank, we cannot count on others to ask us our intentions before they pass judgment. And all our actions are subject to distortion in someone else's frame of reference. This is not to say that no one else's perspective is relevant to understanding our behavior. In fact, it's our differences with others that can provide us with learning situations. But we're especially vulnerable when another person evaluates us before he considers our viewpoint. This lack of justice constitutes one of the biggest deterrents to our gaining control.

One manager has likened evaluation in the organization to evaluation in church. He claimed: "Both set up criteria of performance which I can't possibly measure up to. Both give me a glimpse of perfection I can use for seeing how inadequate I am. Both tell me what constitutes sinfulness, and it includes plenty of what I do. And both tell me that if I act contrite, if I defer, and if I follow the rules, then I won't be judged guilty. If my boss would just make a slave out of me, then life would be simple. But he doesn't; instead he lets me go around seeking absolution. I'm sitting here failing, and he offers me an eleventh commandment, 'Thou shalt be free.' Not only do I have a bag of sins that he knows about, but I'm sitting here worrying about all the ones he's likely to discover tomorrow."

Informally, we're constantly subject to evaluation without having our point of view considered. When it's done by peers and subordinates in the corridors and washrooms of the organization, we experience it as zinging and backbiting. Done by us, a zing can be cathartic, and even fun. But when everybody is doing it, the organization becomes a jungle. As long as we can say whatever we want about fellow workers without considering their point of view or how our needs influence our evaluation, then we're contributing to an organization system in which no one has much control.

Reflection

These are but a few of the traps that keep us from gaining control. Each is based on assumptions we make about how the organization system operates. Raising consciousness about the nature of these traps gives us a chance to improve our organization system.

Geoffrey Vickers' quote at the beginning of this chapter provides a clue to the way out: "The nature of the trap is a function of the nature of the trapped." Not only must we destroy the traps as we find them but we must struggle to understand what in ourselves has made us vulnerable. Ultimately, what we learn in dealing with one trap will help us to avoid others.

The challenge, however, is to get better at seeing our own oppression, no matter how many benefits we seem to have. We've got to stop thinking of control as something other people can give us or as something we can have before we understand what we're doing and why we're doing it. We must probe the hidden aspects of our own experience.

CHAPTER 4

Mantraps
in How We Operate

> Only beings who can reflect upon the fact that they
> are determined are capable of freeing themselves.
> Their reflectiveness results not just in a vague and
> uncommitted awareness, but in the exercise of a
> profoundly transforming action upon the determin-
> ing reality.
>
> Paulo Freire

Not all of the mantraps are found in the assumptions we make about
how the organization system operates. Some are found in the assumptions we make about ourselves and how we operate within the organization. These mantraps, reinforced by others, are the products of our
education and conditioning before we ever went to work for an organization. The effects of these assumptions are the same as the effects of
assumptions we make about how the organization operates: they limit
the extent to which we manage our organization lives, and subject us to
excessive influence by the system.

Each of us makes these assumptions. Some of us more than others,
but we're all conditioned to make them. They're part of our upbringing,
and in the process of living them out, we set traps for ourselves. This
chapter discusses some of these assumptions and the traps they set.

Assumptions That Are Mantraps

• *We assume that we can maintain our own identity despite the
influence of the organization culture in which we're working.* Each of
us believes that he is unique and strong-willed. We know we make

20

compromises in personal style in order to get along with the organization system, but we believe these compromises can always be reversed. We believe that we can go for long periods of time focusing on goals that others hold up for us without losing track of those goals that have primary meaning for us. We also believe that we can immerse ourselves fully in organization life and not be unwittingly influenced in any significant way.

This assumption, like many mantraps, is a variation on the theme of self-determination. It is based on a levelheaded approach to life. It's the part of us that wins the argument but loses the friend, and has the logical explanation for all expressions of feeling. We are reluctant to seek hidden influences that can't readily be identified or focus on known influences that we don't know how to handle. We resist the idea that our behavior is "overdetermined," that more than one reason motivates any given action. While we may concede that unconscious forces influence us, we reason that because they're unconscious, there's little use concerning ourselves with them.

Not understanding when the organization influences our actions results in self-deception for us and wasted manpower for the organization. For example, I recently consulted with a group of accounting managers who were dissatisfied with accounting careers in their company and were seeking to change things. In this company, accounting is considered a rather specialized profession, and accountants aren't considered for managerial roles in other areas. Because few accounting managers had quit or retired, there was a promotion pinch for younger accountants who were trying to get ahead. Men suffering from years of boredom on the same job could only look forward to more of the same. Yet the thought of quitting evoked fear because most of them believed that their company's accounting system was highly specialized and thus didn't feel particularly marketable in what they considered a tight job market.

At my suggestion, the managers agreed to organize themselves into a task force charged with developing a proposal for improving the career opportunities of company accountants. They decided to expand their goals to include issues relevant to the overall effectiveness of the accounting function in their company. They reasoned that dealing only with accounting careers might not contain sufficient incentives for top management to sit up and take notice of their proposal. As it turned out, setting their sights on what top management might think proved to be their undoing.

Task force members interviewed most of the company's top management who had an interest in the accounting function. Not only would top management's perspectives be valuable, they reasoned, but involvement might instill in them feelings of ownership in the results.

Also interviewed was a diverse sampling of people using reports prepared by accountants as well as a sampling of accountants from each company level and work function. They were asked their ideas for improving the quality of accounting work and for upgrading accounting careers. When the interviewing was completed, the managers held study sessions to exchange what they had heard and to decide on a list of recommendations for top management.

While their way of proceeding seemed reasonable enough, the task force turned out to be an exercise in self-deception. Almost all discussions were limited by what the accounting managers thought would be acceptable to top management. Their recommendations did little more than recreate what was acceptable in the past. They emphasized short-term productivity and overlooked most of the knotty issues relative to accounting careers. No basic changes resulted. To me, the sad if understandable thing about the whole business was that the accountants were very excited and pleased with what they had accomplished.

What happened to the accounting managers happens to each of us. It is the predictable consequence of our reluctance to stop what we're doing and question the nature and extent of the forces that are influencing us. We may have our uniqueness in mind when we start a project, but we're continually in danger of being co-opted. It's one thing to know that our individuality is being constrained by external forces of which we're aware; then we know who and what to fight. It's yet another thing to experience external limits that are imposed internally. We seldom recognize the constraints, and when we do, the only person with whom we can fight is ourself.

• *We assume that it's better for us to go along with the organization's story than to hold out for the truth.* Almost daily we're confronted with discrepancies between what a representative of the organization says is taking place and what we, by virtue of our own experience, know is happening. When the misperception is held collectively by a group or by someone with power, we think, "It's easier not to make an issue," "All I'll do is get in a fight," and "Who's going to change his mind anyway?" We reason, "It doesn't make that much difference who else knows what's really going on; the important thing is that I know what's taking place."

I've seen this assumption exposed numerous times when, as a consultant, I sit in on group meetings between a newly appointed boss and his subordinates. Subordinates at that time are willing to tell how with their former boss they suppressed the truth about how they operated, ignored the boss's shortcomings, and pretended to go along with the prescribed way. The new boss gains security from subordinates taking him into their confidence, the subordinates get years of frustration off their chests, and everyone acts as if it's impossible for the same mess to be repeated. But there's no discussion about how this pattern might be changed. Thus, the only thing it's safe to predict is that some day these subordinates will be sitting around telling the same stories to another new boss who, like his predecessor, will have missed hearing what he needs to hear if he's to improve the organization and learn from past mistakes.

The companies whose stock we buy and the savings banks we use are subtle examples of our need to go along with the organization's story. As long as we think they're using our money for worthwhile purposes, we can relax. Once we learn that the companies are making their profits from worthless cold remedies and the banks are slum landlords, then we've got some choices to make, choices that may be inconsistent with our investment and banking needs. As long as we believe that the men at the top of our organization are benevolent and infinitely wise, we can relax. But once we start taking our discrepant experiences seriously and see that executives need to be questioned, we *have* to accept new responsibilities and start worrying about how to act on our own perceptions.

Here's an example of an executive who let the truth slide for thirty-seven years, but didn't really forget. The truth came out at his retirement dinner. It was a heavy drinking party, and the retiring executive, named Charlie, got pretty looped. When the master of ceremonies presented the watch, Charlie staggered forward to express his thanks. He said, "I've waited years to talk about what's been going on in this company. Now that I'm leaving, I am going to have my say." He then went into thirty minutes of facts. He told how a number of top officers were squeezed out, why the company had to discontinue manufacturing some of its most popular products, and a few juicy stories about who was sleeping with whom. The audience sat numbed through the entire expurgation. When Charlie finished, he slumped down, and the white-faced company president stood up, gathered his composure, and said briskly, "Thanks, Charlie, for your thoughtful words of candor." He then went back to his script, extolling Charlie for his years of accomplishment and service. When he finished, he went over to shake Charlie's hand. Charlie stood, apparently unaware that he had given his speech, and launched into another thirty minutes of the same facts.

• *We assume that heightened self-consciousness and self-examination will create more personal problems than it solves.* This is one assumption that most of us wish weren't true, but see no way of getting around. Self-analysis produces pain and raises anxiety that interferes with our work performance. We don't seem able to analyze our personal problems objectively. We're not able to balance our strengths and weaknesses as we can with a technical problem or when weighing the pros and cons of driving the scenic versus the fast route to San Francisco. Thus, when we face a problem in our performance, we'd rather blame externals, events and other people, than examine our personal contribution.

Each of us has problem-solving styles, work patterns, and interaction styles that seem to characterize us in our organization life. While these patterns are fairly predictable to those who know us best, we usually avoid thinking about them. Part of our avoidance stems from our not wanting to see how these patterns violate our ideals. Another part comes from our knowing that we are more complex than others give us credit for and that there's no reason to get too upset by some criticism that doesn't always apply. However, the times when we're most open to modifying our patterns are the times when we're the least flexible. Only during times of crisis do we seem willing to try another way. But time pressures, anxieties, and feelings of failure at these same moments work against us. We become defensive and can't seem to concentrate on examining our motives, even though we're willing to change our behavior. And when the crisis lifts, we're comfortably back at our old ways.

This assumption gets in our way when we least want it to. Others notice our foibles despite our own desire to keep them hidden. They use them to stereotype us because it's the part of us that gets in *their* way. In other people's minds, we're dangerous or inept. Each of us knows numerous instances of how others spot a lack of self-awareness and penalize that person for it.

For example, there is an upper-level manager who has the reputation of being fun to work with for aggressive, quick-witted people, but is a treacherous associate for weak, less aggressive people. From the manager's standpoint, he treats all people the same, but he's at his most creative when using an argumentative style that bothers less aggressive people. These people feel that he just wants to listen to his own ideas, so there's no reason for them to expose their best arguments for him to destroy.

I know a middle-level manager who was disappointed to learn that a promotion that had been promised was withdrawn, because he seemed unable to explain adequately work assignments to his subordinates. From his standpoint, he disliked making excessive demands of people and tried to approach his staff democratically. The result was that neither his boss nor his subordinates had much respect for his leadership, although everyone liked him as a person.

There is a television writer who predictably gets into fights with directors, producers, and writer colleagues. From her standpoint, they're always nice at the beginning, but when they find out how talented she is, they become uptight and jealous. From their standpoint, she comes on very feminine and dependent at first, but as soon as they try to give her some help, she becomes hostile and cutting.

One last anecdote is hardly believable, but it's true. It involves a forty-eight-year-old social science researcher who was studying productivity peaks among middle-aged employees and was fired for lack of productivity himself.

None of these stories are important by themselves, but as the same dynamics are repeated over the course of a person's life, the importance of self-understanding and heightened consciousness become apparent. Any single episode can be dismissed or blamed solely on external events and people. However, as they recur, with many different situations and people, we begin to see the importance of identifying our own contributions.

• *We assume that we can deal with our problems individually without relating them to the problems faced by others in similar situations.* We are individuals and want to be treated that way. We prize our own identity and don't want to settle for less than first-person consideration of our concerns and interests. We know ourselves the best, and, accordingly, we should be able to do the best job of negotiating a suitable role. Tying our fate to a group involves unnecessary compromises and problems, the solutions to which may not even help us personally. In this context, a middle manager said to me "I can't solve the problems I've got, what am I going to do with everyone elses."

This assumption works when the person we're dealing with has only us in mind. But if he's worrying about what others will demand after he gives in to us, we're not going to fare so well. Meanwhile, we're experiencing ambivalence between wanting to be part of a group while remaining an individual. For instance, an upper-level manager told me recently: "I have a Jonathan Livingston Seagull complex. I get upset when a peer progresses faster than me. This is a blow to my ego. But when I get into a philosophical mood, I start wondering, 'Am I in free flight, or am I part of the flock? Am I winging it, or am I held back by my concern for the group?' "

In this connection, I remember a conversation I once had with an associate after he had advised me that "Bill is in trouble with the system." "Why is it," I wanted to know, "that people are always in trouble with the system? When something goes wrong, why not consider the possibility that it is the system that is in trouble?" My associate answered, "Because the system is so much bigger."

The trap embodied in this assumption can produce the worst type of naïveté. Recently, I was talking to an administrative systems man who was upset that men working at comparable levels in other staff groups within his company were being paid 33 percent more than he was. He was all charged up to confront his boss and demand a raise. I pointed out that other members in his department were also being paid less and questioned whether he might not get farther by considering the systemwide consequences of this inequity. The man replied that his competence was a cut above most administrative systems men and that he could do much better on his own.

I agreed that this man was underpaid, competent, and deserving of a big raise. But by not associating himself with the group, he was passing up a chance to strengthen the overall functioning of the organization. As it turned out, the man didn't fare too well. He walked into Phase III pay guidelines and got only a 5 percent increase and a pat on the back. He paid a price too, for now he's vulnerable to resentment if his colleagues find out about his raise.

In effect, this man exchanged the potential benefits of group identity for a very small gain. He's negotiating as an individual with an organization that sees him as a member of a group. How can he help but be out-muscled?

• *We assume that we can avoid conflicts between our allegiances to different groups by reasoning that what's good for our work team is good and what's bad for the team is bad.* If we worry about everyone, we'll never get anything accomplished. We can't concern ourselves with every issue and cause. We've got to focus somewhere, and the most logical place is with the projects of our work team. This assumption, which we incorporate while we're very young and express throughout our work life, is the backbone of the competitive system. It leads to technological progress and economic prosperity, but it also results in redundancy and worthless projects. This team concept of excellence admires individual accomplishment primarily for its contribution to the success of the team. At its root is the double edge of ethnocentrism, whereby one group's cohesiveness and *esprit de corps* are accomplished by having a common enemy; thus, there is *intra*team collaboration because of the pressures of *inter*team competition.

It is this assumption that can lead entire marketing groups to misrepresent their products, even though the consumers they thus mislead include members of their own organization and families. Similarly, this assumption leads groups to withhold information from other groups in the same organization, even though the company's profits depend on the success of all groups. More generally this assumption leads to contaminated air and water, even though those who contribute to this contamination live in the affected areas.

Yet *not* assuming our work team is all-important creates trouble for us. If we raise our allegiances up a level to the good of the larger society, we lose our own security and economic gain. Farmers can help fight inflation by keeping down costs and settling for a lower margin of profit. Politicians can contribute to the democratic system by placing more emphasis on the conduct of campaigns rather than on the victory of candidates. Managers of federal agencies can eliminate units that have outlived their purpose, even if it means reducing the visibility and power of their organizations. Technicians can share information broadly, without concern for who gets the credit. While we don't like the consequences of the system produced by people holding narrow allegiances, raising our allegiance to a higher plane jeopardizes lower-level needs.

The problems created by an allegiance to the work team are often so subtle that the work group involved has no idea of what's taking place. For example, recently the number of children available for adoption in our country has dropped considerably. Logically, this should result in staff cutbacks by the adoption agencies. But in at least one agency I know of, it led instead to changes in accounting procedures and counseling techniques so that there were few staff cutbacks. By shifting the reporting system from the number of cases handled to the number of hours spent on each case, the staff seems as busy as ever, and they are, but the counseling philosophy has also changed. Adoption workers once encouraged natural mothers to keep their children. Now they encourage mothers to take a hard look at the conflicts in living a life with a child about whom she feels ambivalent.

None of us can be counted on to remain conscious of the cause we're serving when our allegiance is to a particular work team, nor the higher order opportunities we're neglecting by holding on to this allegiance. If we could, then there would be no mantrap here.

• *We assume that we're being productive as long as we're physically busy and completing projects.* We like to see results and dislike periods of grueling planning and lonely reflection. We're part of an action-oriented culture. Anxiety and frustration quickly build up when we go too long without producing *something*; we don't even mind working on projects we know will be wiped out and forgotten in a few days.

Yet the problems we work on are often so complex that they take a long time to complete, and daily progress is impossible to measure. So we invent diversionary activities and devise meaningless benchmarks against which progress can be assessed. Some people find accomplishment in the number of hours they work. They feel good if they can say, "Yesterday I put in twelve hours at the office and two and a half hours of briefcase work at home." Even paper shuffling has its rewards. We measure our accomplishment by the number of inches in the out basket. A manager once confided, "When I see I'm getting ahead of the pile, I go out and talk to my secretary so I don't have to face the problem of what to do when I run out of work."

When someone works long hours without tangible output, he has a tendency to get in other people's hair. This phenomenon was commented upon by a colleague who's consulting specialty is in research and development organizations. He contends that each research and development manager needs a project that's like a mistress, so that when he gets bored he has someplace to screw around besides the laboratories of the people working for him.

I know of any number of instances where a man's need to see accomplishment was met at the expense of the organization's effectiveness and relevance. One in particular concerns a technical manager who was called in to solve a supervisory problem created when unit chiefs could not control the effectiveness of technical specialists reporting to them. The manager faced a frustrating task because the specialists were reluctant to give up the autonomy and independence they had acquired during this managerial void. They weren't about to let anybody scrutinize their activities.

As it turned out, the specialists had built sufficiently strong relationships with their unit chiefs to enable them to withstand the manager's attempt to coordinate and supervise their activities. Eventually, the manager quit trying. He told me, "I've gotten so fed up working on coordination that I've gone back to doing work in my own unit. Now I get satisfaction because I'm outcome-oriented. Even though I'm avoiding what I'm supposed to be doing, I feel good about how much I'm accomplishing." I replied, "Yes, but there's a cost." He interrupted, "The cost is that nobody is doing the coordination work, but then you'd have to be an idiot to keep trying with this group." What else was there for me to say? However, from the standpoint of the organization, an essential job still is not being done.

Reflection

Few if any of the assumptions we make about ourselves and how we operate were acquired in the organization. Rather, they are what we bring to the organization. Indeed, they are what makes it work the way it does.

Too many of these assumptions keep us from even seeing what's wrong with the way we're living our organization life, let alone from positioning ourselves to change it. To the extent that our assumptions are wrong, incomplete, or don't relate to the specific context in which they're being applied, they limit our control. Because everyone believes in them, it's not likely we'll get much support from others in debunking them. The irony is that almost everyone has had, at one time or another, an occasion to see the limitations of these assumptions. Typically, these limitations are apparent only when observed in someone else's life. When we can see how they are manifest in our own life, then we will have learned something useful.

PART II

Understanding the
Traps We're In

CHAPTER 5

What Makes a Trap

One strategy for coping with mantraps involves identifying them and digging our way out. However, this strategy still leaves us susceptible to entanglement in a new set of traps. We could spend a lifetime falling into traps and digging out without ever exerting positive direction over our activities in the organization. Ultimately, we've got to learn some basics that will help us to avoid new traps.

Each of the mantraps we've been discussing reflects our inability to understand something basic about what it means to have a choice, to have an alternative, and to take responsibility. We go along unable to recognize a choice that expresses our individuality from one that subtly manipulates us; we are dependent on others to present us with alternatives because we can't formulate them for ourselves; and our life in the organization is constrained by a self-defeating definition of responsibility.

What we need to understand is not particularly complex, but it does require some abstract thinking about our life in the organization. We need to analyze each specific action we contemplate for its elements of choice, alternative, and responsibility. Such analysis will help us dig out from existing mantraps as well as enable us to avoid new ones.

Choice

We can learn to distinguish between an option that actually gives us choice and an option that cloaks the fact that we have little choice. For instance, there are choices that stem from what someone else wants us to do rather than from what we want to do for ourselves. In such cases, the process of choosing becomes little more than our trying to guess what others will think and then performing in a way that insures they will get the right impression.

For example, I was sitting with a department head and his top-level staff as they reassessed the department's philosophy of operations. Every hour or so, a secretary would walk into our conference room with a note asking the department head to return a phone call to his boss, who was a company vice-president. I couldn't imagine any activity more crucial to the running of this man's department than what was taking place in the room he kept leaving. At lunch, I buttonholed him and asked, "Ted must have quite a crisis?" He replied, "No, nothing that couldn't wait till next week." I said, "Then why haven't you left word that you'll call him back when our meeting is over?" He answered, "If it's important enough for Ted to call, then it's more important than what I'm doing." While this department head had a choice when to return Ted's call, apparently he thought only one response was "organizationally correct."

There are choices in which the options are equally unsatisfactory. These involve options formulated for us by someone else. It's the choice a manager had when he told his boss he'd like to change secretaries and the boss replied, "Fine, you can have my Miss Martin," the boss's secretary with whom he had long been dissatisfied. It's the choice we get when our main medical expense is for the family dentist and we're asked to select between two medical insurance plans, neither of which have dental coverage.

There is the choice about an issue that is fairly low on our personal list of priorities. This is the choice we get when our boss gathers our entire work unit together to decide on next year's vacation schedule and we're still trying to find the time to use up the days we're entitled to this year. It is the choice we get when we're working for a large organization that promotes slowly and trains thoroughly and we're asked what we'd like to learn next when what we really want is to get a job that finally gives us some responsibility with a commensurate raise in pay.

There are choices in which we are asked to decide between a single option and an uncertainty, without any assurance that we'll get another opportunity if we turn it down. This type of choice leads us to accept an additional committee assignment when we're already overloaded, because we don't know when we'll get another chance to receive this type of recognition and visibility or to work with these attractive people. This type of choice leads us to violate something we believe in, like the continuity of our children's schooling, because we don't know when we'll get another chance to spend two years working in South America.

None of the above choices affords us a real option, each really usurps our autonomy. We're likely to think we're making decisions when we're really trying to optimize rewards and limit punishments within a set of externally imposed constraints.

Let's take a close look at how this kind of choice works in a particular situation. This example involves an engineer who was asked to supervise a three-month-long project in a city one hundred and fifty miles from his home. The engineer and his boss reasoned that the duration of the assignment was sufficiently short that he might do it as a temporary commute. This would entail a three-and-a-half-hour train ride, leaving home early Monday morning and returning home late Friday evening. By commuting, he would avoid disrupting the schooling of his four children and save the company the added expense of a short-term move. The engineer assumed that the assignment was his rite of passage to a promotion. His family's sacrifice would be offset by the rewards of the promotion that would follow his demonstration of competence and loyalty to the company.

The assignment, however, turned into a disaster. It was extended, by mutual agreement, one month at a time for twenty-two months. As the months wore on, the engineer first got furious with himself and later angry at the company, although he couldn't quite figure out why the company was to blame. He felt he was a big boy and the choice was his own. He didn't realize that from at least one perspective he had made a nonchoice. As long as he wanted the promotion and remained ignorant of other ways he might earn it, he had but a single option; there was no real choice to make.

A deception of this magnitude certainly represents a collusion between the man and the organization. But when I separately interviewed the engineer and his wife, neither was aware of their roles in creating this situation or in perpetuating it when it had clearly gotten out of hand. Parenthetically, you might wonder whether or not the engineer's self-deception paid off. It's hard to say because the engineer wasn't promoted until two years later, after he had the chance to demonstrate his competence again on another important project.

For the engineer to have a real choice, he should have known the probability of promotion following his sacrifice as well as any other options available to show his worth and be promoted. For the family to have had a choice, they should have known the probability for the project lasting longer than planned and how much longer. With such perspectives they could have exercised options and shared risks. Certainly, the engineer was as guilty as the company in not providing them with this perspective. Even if a company representative gave him the wrong estimate, he was quite capable of going out and sizing up the situation for himself.

Ultimately, we want to create real choices for ourselves. First, this means recognizing when we have options but no real choice. Next, it means knowing enough about the characteristics of choice to know which options actually reflect our interests. Finally, a real choice should offer us a chance to express our own taste and style, not just to optimize rewards and minimize costs and punishments. Specifically, having choice means that:

1. We're choosing from two or more options and are aware of them; thus, we're not choosing between a single known and an unknown.
2. The options are different ways to accomplish the same objective; thus, we're choosing between options that, in practice, are mutually exclusive.
3. The issue to which the options relate has meaning to us, not just to the people who are presenting them to us; thus, we're choosing something that affects our happiness or expresses our personal style.
4. How we choose is not excessively influenced by others in the organization; thus, we're not involved in trying to guess what "they" are counting on us to do.
5. The options open to us are based on the same assumption about our relationship to the organization; thus, if someone offers us a choice between "privileges," then the privileges from which we're selecting should not include "rights" we're entitled to anyway.
6. The options we're choosing from leave us better off than when we started; thus, choosing isn't a matter of merely trying to minimize costs.
7. The benefits of making a choice are worth the costs, thus, we're not using up a choice on something of little consequence that we could spend later on an issue of greater personal meaning.

Making a real choice depends on our ability to identify each option open to us and to understand the life issue involved in our decision.

If we take a passive stance, we can't count on getting a real choice. Others will, in good faith, present us with options that don't do much for us. Being active involves analyzing the options and not totally depending on any organization, no matter how benevolent its managerial philosophy. Sometimes people will pose options that constitute important opportunities for us to express our own style and taste. However, we'll never know when to trust them unless we put their options to *our* own test.

Alternatives

When is a choice an alternative? In practice, this is one of the most difficult questions we have to answer to gain more control. In theory, however, it's not particularly complex.

Choices confront us with different ways to accomplish a single objective. Alternatives confront us with different objectives.

Choices are based on the same assumption about our relationship with the organization and thus give us a chance to express our own style and taste. Alternatives are based on different assumptions about our relationship with the organization and thus give us a chance to assert something new which is fundamental to our identity.

Alternatives, in other words, *are options based on different assumptions about our relationship with an organization, where one approximates our nature and/or ideals more closely than the relationship we're currently living.* Most frequently the alternatives are between precedent and innovation, occasionally they are two newly created options.

The first step in formulating alternatives is to bring to the surface the assumptions we make about our relationship to the organization, assumptions that are implicit in the different options that we contemplate. Too often the options we contemplate are in fact based on the same assumption and, while we may have a definite preference for one option, neither appreciably changes our relationship with the organization. For example, the engineer who commuted for twenty-two months had no alternative as long as, in the short run, he viewed his relationship with the organization as one in which he needed to get ahead. If other options for promotion had been made available to him, then he'd have had a real choice but not an alternative. He could *choose* which option involved the least sacrifice. However, as long as his mind was set primarily on getting ahead, no option could be an alternative.

What would an alternative look like? Consider some of the assumptions that link most organization systems with the managers who work for them and the managers' families:

1. Good organization managers should be able to manage their families . . . this translates to "keep family concerns out of the organization's hair."
2. The family is the ultimate benefactor of job success . . . this translates to "family interests come second to those of the organization."
3. Deferred living today will bring richer living tomorrow . . . this translates to "one should strive to live better tomorrow even if it means making substantial sacrifices in the quality of living today."

A manager who works in an organization that makes such assumptions can develop alternatives only after he gains sufficient understanding of his own nature to know when these assumptions do not fit his life priorities. Only then can he be sensitive to options that come closer to expressing his own priorities, let alone envision alternatives that he could suggest to the organization.

Few options that we encounter strike directly at the core of our nature. Even if one did we'd probably dismiss it as utterly impractical. In all likelihood, the alternatives we identify will be only incrementally closer to our nature and ideals. If we're fortunate enough to put one alternative into practice, it should in turn pave the way to our being able to recognize the next.

Occasionally, an alternative is formulated for us by the organization; more often, it's up to us to formulate alternatives for ourselves. For example, a manager might know that the demands of that new position he is being offered have done in able men before him. If he declines this promotion on the grounds that he'd like to go home at night and relax, then he would be exercising an alternative. But if he takes the promotion, assuming that he can resist the pressures of the job, and time shows his assumption to be self-deluding, then he will have lost control because he has been acting on an unrealistic assumption about his abilities. Another example of a self-formulated alternative would be a manager who realizes that he enjoys doing his own technical work more than supervising the technical work of others and decides to return to his technical specialty.

Intelligently meeting the options that occur in organization life requires that we understand the assumptions on which they are based and that we have sufficient self-knowledge to recognize which assumption comes closest to reflecting who we are. Limitations in self-knowledge also limit our ability to formulate or recognize alternatives, whether they are posed by ourselves or by others. Later chapters of this book will show how we can bring these assumptions out into the open so that we can decide which alternatives fit us best.

Responsibility

Our consideration of mantraps has already suggested what's wrong with the way we define responsibility in our organization life. Responsibility in this sense typically means standing accountable for the actions we take or don't take, even when we have little understanding of the forces directing us. It means making sure that the organization's prevailing ways influence the way we operate, even though we have little understanding of how they came into being. This definition of responsibility tells others when they are morally justified in punishing us. It tells us what principles we must feel guilty about violating.

Defining responsibility in this way often leads to our being punished for actions we never understood or which seemed natural enough at the time we took them. In being thus held accountable, we usually learn little that helps us to understand what was going on or how to improve our performance when the same basic issue presents itself in another context.

We can characterize this definition of responsibility as *after-the-fact* accountability and contrast it with a new one that emphasizes *before-the-fact* consciousness. This new definition challenges us to understand the forces that prompted us to act the way we did, even if we have to figure this out in retrospect. It's not enough to say, "I wasn't promoted because I lack initiative." We also need to learn the areas where we fail to initiate and the reasons why we have such difficulty. And we need to know all of this before things get so bad that people can never see us any other way.

This new type of responsibility holds us accountable to ourselves, not just to others. However, as long as we choose to live in the social context of the organization world, we cannot neglect the meaning our actions hold for others who have importance for us. But the name of the game is awareness, and this may mean frustrating the desires of others. If someone wants to criticize us for not writing a report, it's one thing to respond, "I didn't know that's what you wanted," and it's another thing to be able to say, "I knew what you wanted, but I didn't think writing it would do much for any of us."

In summary, the emphasis is on determining what forces influence us before we act. Identifying these forces, even after-the-fact, is essential to responsible action. Now let's expand this conception of responsibility to encompass what's been discussed about choice and alternative. Responsibility in the context of organization life means:

1. Understanding what we're doing, or not doing, and why it needs to be done, or not done.
2. Understanding the meaning our actions are likely to hold for others, outside the organization as well as inside.
3. Figuring out whether or not an option actually constitutes a choice about how to proceed.
4. Realizing which assumptions about our relationship to the organization are contained in two choices and determining whether either choice constitutes an alternative or merely another way of accomplishing the same objective.
5. Increasing our self-awareness so that we can determine the extent to which we're choosing alternatives consistent with who we are and/or who we'd like to be rather than reaffirming the identity that the organization has selected for us.

Reflection

These conceptualizations of choice, alternative, and responsibility enable us to move directly to a more detailed consideration of what it means to gain control of our organization life. However, it's important to remember that control over one's organization life is not something others can give us, no matter how much they may love us, value us, or want only what's best for us. Control is something we must get for ourselves, and the best others can do is to be aboveboard so we can spot the assumptions implicit in our relationship with them and the organization. The rest is up to us.

CHAPTER 6

How We've Been Conditioned To Respond

> In the last analysis, the question of what are true and false needs must be answered by the individuals themselves, but only in the last analysis; that is, if and when they are free to give their own answer. As long as they are kept incapable of being autonomous, as long as they are indoctrinated and manipulated (down to their very instincts), their answer to this question cannot be taken as their own.
>
> Herbert Marcuse

By now it should be clear that there's more to being in control than merely being able to take action as we see fit. We can make choices that are inconsequential, we can act without expressing something fundamental in our nature, and we can fulfill organization roles without understanding the purpose behind what we're doing. Until we can focus on our pictures of reality that lead us to think, choose, and decide the way we do, we'll be hard pressed to know when it is something basic in us and not some external force that's behind our actions.

How we see the world is largely the result of how we've been conditioned to fit into the organization, and much of this teaching has been implicit. Usually, we respond emotionally to our lesson and fail to consider whether or not what we have learned will interfere with our desires to express ourselves in our organization life. Our instruction is as casual as a colleague's crack about who we were eating lunch with yesterday and as deliberate as a boss's appraisal of our work.

Most frequently we walk away from a lesson, focusing on the external rewards and punishments while neglecting the internal. We think, "That's the last time I'll ever do that," or, "Now I know what they want from me," or, "Next time I'll make sure they get the right impression." Only infrequently do we think, "There's something important about not yielding completely on this one, although I can't quite put my finger on what it is," or, "I've got to go back and show them that it's only because they want to keep operating the same way that they need me to change."

Our vulnerability to conditioning has been extreme, and consequently, we've lost some things that are essential to our identity. For example, an executive vice-president of a large corporation explained to a division manager that he would never make vice-president because he was too rough in his dealings with top-level brass. Can you guess what type of response that evoked? A very long-winded, emotional "I'll change." The division manager offered to change without much conscious reflection of what he had been trying to accomplish over the years with his "no-bullshit" style. After all, this was the same style that earned him the senior position he occupied.

We accept too much of what happens to us without understanding how it is the product of our conditioning. For instance, I know a group of eleven college graduates recently hired to be manufacturing managers in a multiplant manufacturing organization. Each is frustrated because he has yet to talk with the plant manager. While they have been moaning about this for six months, their "constructive" action has been limited to voicing their dissatisfaction during weekly conferences with their immediate supervisors.

There are many ways to describe the problem faced by these young managers. We could term it a problem of reporting to an insensitive and overscheduled plant manager. I prefer to see it as a problem of excessive conditioning. These young managers don't know how to get what they need. Apparently they are so in awe of authority, so respectful of organization protocol, and so afraid of peer-group competition that they can't envision alternative solutions, even though they've had time to see that their moaning hasn't payed off. For instance, I asked the plant manager what would happen if these guys got together and arranged a meeting to which they invited him. He replied, "That would constitute an offer I couldn't refuse."

The process that conditions us in the beliefs, rules, and values of a social system is called socialization. This process is most clearly seen, and therefore most thoroughly studied, as children grow up in an existing society. But the same type of process occurs when we are inducted into an organization. Usually, socialization is accomplished through implicit teaching, and this can cause us problems. The people instructing us aren't aware of what they're teaching us, and we're not aware of what we're learning. Some of what we take in doesn't fit at the time we learn it, and some no longer applies to who we become or what we eventually do. All this puts us out of control while thinking we're in control.

Thus, socialization shapes our picture of reality without our knowing it. Until we understand how the external forces of our socialization have influenced our pictures of the organization world, we cannot exert any real control. Developing this understanding requires some kind of consciousness-raising process. We can begin by identifying and reassessing which basic assumptions direct our actions. For instance, the young managers, mentioned above, need to reassess the assumptions they made about going through channels in light of their feeling alienated from their organization's power structure.

Contrasting the assumptions implied by our actions with what we know through our experience gives us a chance to reaffirm and commit ourselves to valid assumptions and to identify and reject assumptions that don't fit. The most important opportunities for gaining control occur when we hit upon an invalid assumption. This not only gives us a chance to set ourselves straight but it also helps us see in what way we're vulnerable to social conditioning.

There are psychological principles that explain when we're particularly susceptible to social conditioning. Thus, we know that a marginal member of a group identifies most closely and least flexibly with the beliefs of that group. We know that someone under intense pressure will gradually distort his perceptions until these pressures are reduced to a tolerable level. We know that a person who is being tyrannized, without opportunity to escape, is inclined to identify with those he sees as the source of his oppression. And we know that a person looks for authority figures to admire and identify with, particularly when he's in a crisis, rising to a challenge, or unsure of his own identity. Overall, we know that each of us is most vulnerable to socialization when he's highly anxious and involved in unfamiliar or ambiguous situations.

Consciousness-raising begins by identifying an assumption and recalling the events and circumstances that were present when we first made it. Subtleties that eluded us at the time can often be seen in retrospect. The validity of an assumption rests partly on an accurate perception of the people and organization system involved and partly on whether or not comparable situations, psychological needs, and external conditions exist today.

In a sense, consciousness-raising brings old pictures of reality up to date. We identify assumptions that have been directing our lives. We reconstruct the conditions that existed when we first learned them, and determine whether the assumptions still apply. We try to identify the situations and conditions in which we're particularly susceptible. And we try to replace assumptions that no longer seem suitable with ones that better fit current experience. If the term socialization describes the formative process we've been through, then the term self-directed resocialization describes the process we're attempting to create. Essentially, we're struggling to become the architects of our own destiny.

Reflection

Replacing old pictures of reality with new ones that fit us better will at times put us at odds with the organization. Negotiating these conflicts will require energy and additional skills—not to mention support. Organizations dislike self-initiated change because it seems to rock the boat. While organizations can't shut off our energy to raise consciousness, they can, and have in the past, successfully block us from developing the support to do this well. Part III will present guidelines for recruiting such support as well as for developing the skills to be successful. However, even with support and skills, the quality of our consciousness-raising is contingent on what we can learn from our daily experience.

CHAPTER 7

Overcoming
Simplistic
Pictures of Reality

Understanding where our pictures of reality come from is one of two consciousness-raising activities essential to gaining control of our organization life. The other entails learning the lessons of our experience and using what we learn to improve the quality of the pictures directing us. We want to be confident that our pictures reflect our own needs and interests and we want them to be based on a realistic view of the organization and what we're doing in it. We need to develop a more complex and objective picture of reality so that we can recognize opportunities to live a personally meaningful organization life and comprehend how our activities are relevant to organization goals. In particular, we need greater understanding about ourselves, who we are and what our ideals are; about the organization, what it is and how it actually works; and about the relationship we have formed with the organization.

The importance of adding complexity and objectivity to our pictures of reality can be seen in the issues faced by Pete, a marketing expert. Pete is a standout performer, but periodically he works on projects that get botched up. In Pete's mind, some soft-minded boss's failure to supervise effectively screwed things up. Marketing managers who have supervised him have learned the hard way that failures can usually be traced back to Pete's letting up when a project was under pressure. They say they've been unsuccessful in discussing this with Pete because he always sees it as their fault.

Pete will have a choice when he can reflect on his experiences, see the patterns he's been living, and bring into the open the assumptions implied by his actions. He can use his experience to learn about himself, as he actually is, about his dependence on forceful leadership, and about how the organization values people who work well with minimal supervision, regardless of project pressures. Additionally, he can use his experience to learn about his relationship with the organization, that he's been labeled as a guy who requires a great deal of direct supervision and handholding. Such an understanding of the image he projects could help him set other people's expectations straight, or he might resolve to learn how to depend less on direct guidance or he might decide that changing isn't worth the personal hassle. In any event, learning the lessons contained in his experience would allow Pete to exert greater control over his organization life. But, to my knowledge, Pete has yet to make these connections.

In this failure to make connections, each of us is like Pete. Our experience already contains lessons that we don't know how to use, and we have the capacity to learn much more than we typically do. Even when we know better, we try to get away with simplifying a problem, as Pete does when a project goes sour. He has yet to learn some critical things about himself, and he's failed to appreciate the complexity of those who supervise him.

We too frequently oversimplify others. We resist thinking that they are as complex, thorough, and flexible as we know ourselves to be. For instance, I recently assisted in planning a meeting that sought to iron out the tensions between a sales and an advertising group. I suggested that the recently replaced promotion manager be invited because he had played a role in producing these tensions, and the sorting out might teach him a few things he could put to use in his new assignment. The people planning this meeting said, "That's a good idea, but *Jerry* couldn't take it." It always seems to be the other guy who can't take it, can't learn, or possesses an immutable flaw in his character.

We can increase the complexity and objectivity of our pictures of reality if we remember that similar experiences produce different pictures. How often have we found out after a meeting was over that the person sitting next to us saw the same events quite differently. Our typical reaction is to point out how the other guy missed what was actually going on. When this difference in perception takes place in a large group, it's relatively easy for us to shrug our shoulders and forget about it. But when it happens in a small meeting, say with just one other person, it can be unnerving.

However, on a good day, such different perceptions can provide us with unusual opportunities for learning. I say "a good day" because facing such differences creates anxiety, and there are days when we just can't take additional pressures and have no use for one more lesson. But when we're ready for learning, we can take note of the difference and begin looking for past experiences that explain why we saw things so differently. I know of two managers, with comparable responsibilities in the same company, who sat down to figure out why one had been motivated to institute a job-bidding system and the other had not. Their ground rules barred them from debating the pros and cons of job bidding. Rather, the focus was on understanding why they felt so differently about it. They began their discussion at two in the afternoon, continued through dinner, and wound up talking into the night. Their difference provided them with a vehicle for learning more about themselves, the way their company actually worked, and the types of relationships each had formed with the company.

Learning lessons from other people's experience is an easy way to supplement what we're able to get directly. There's no need to learn everything from the "school of hard knocks." We can learn about experiences we've yet to have and about lessons we've yet to have. Of course, we'll also be exposed to many perspectives that are based on experiences we'll never have and that result not from the other person's direct experience but from what he was conditioned to believe. But even in these instances, we can't intelligently dismiss someone else's perspective until we uncover the experiences that led to his particular conclusions.

Whether or not a single objective picture of reality exists is unimportant. What *is* important is that a changing and more complex picture of reality almost always exists, and gaining control of our organization life depends on our constantly asking the questions that will allow us to discover it. Situations and people change, and what's complex and relevant today won't be tomorrow. We must see to it that our reality pictures keep pace.

Debilitating insularity, derived from living with fixed pictures of reality, is epitomized to my mind at least, in retirement communities like Sun City, where residents seek a "planned" environment that shields them from encounters with a complex world. Such communities play on people's insecurities and on the mistaken belief that they can live a vital life without confronting different realities. People who live there run the risk of having their pictures of reality deteriorate in quality. Some residents have complained that, even within their well-structured, self-contained, homogeneous environment, things are changing too rapidly. Changes in the wrong direction, perhaps. But too fast?

Most of us, however, live in heterogeneous environments that constantly bombard us with different perspectives on reality. For us, maintaining our focus depends upon our ability to identify external influences when they are present. We can't stop others from trying to influence us, and, besides, who wants to go it alone. But we must keep checking our pictures of reality for excessive tampering. It's not enough that we know what we like. We also must know why we like it and whether or not it's in our best interests.

Reflection

Essentially, we've been discussing the importance of raising our consciousness by explicating and adding depth to the reality pictures directing us. This type of consciousness is the basic ingredient for gaining control of our organization life. Greater consciousness will help us to size up situations accurately, to develop greater self-awareness, to understand the real workings of the organization, and to comprehend the relationships we've formed with the organization system.

CHAPTER 8

Why We Are Susceptible: Our Need for Acceptance

- How did we become so susceptible to external influences?
- What makes us so vulnerable to implicit conditioning?
- Why do we subordinate knowledge from our own experiences to realities that others hold up for us?
- Why do we get so defensive when others think differently than we do?
- Why do we fail to expand our pictures of reality to include the lessons of new experiences?

Each of these questions tries to get at the reasons why certain aspects of experience consistently elude our conscious recognition. Apparently, some universal aspect of our needs and motivations renders us vulnerable to external controls. If we could identify the internal mechanism that prevents us from knowing when we're out of control, then we would understand our vulnerability.

A complete picture of man's needs and motivations would take us far beyond the scope of this book. Theories that do this already exist. Freud, Erikson, Fenichel, Reich, Maslow, Rogers, and others have written comprehensively to explain our psychological functioning and personality styles. Of this group, I find the theories of Carl Rogers*

* Rogers' ideas are best expressed in "A theory of therapy, personality and interpersonal relationships, as developed in the client-centered framework," in *Psychology: A study of science*, ed. S. Koch, vol. 3 (New York: McGraw-Hill, 1959).

the most useful in explaining our susceptibility to the traps of organization life. His concepts are easy to understand, and his formulation of how a child develops contains useful ideas that can help us exert greater influence over our socialization process.

Rogers' theory of socialization, although he doesn't call it this, emphasizes the conditioning that takes place in infancy and early childhood. This is the time when we were first exposed to the pressures of adapting our needs to an existing social order, when our dependencies and self-doubts were first established, and when we learned the defenses that today protect us from the anxiety that these dependencies and self-doubts created.

While defenses reduce anxiety, they do so by distorting and narrowing our pictures of reality. They protect us but only at the expense of our becoming overly vulnerable to external influences. By developing a perspective on what we're protecting, we can overcome this vulnerability and make our pictures of reality less susceptible to the implicit shaping by others.

According to Rogers, all infants are born with a need for self-regard and a tendency to value all instinctual and pleasurable experiences. At first, the infant can't differentiate himself from the environment, but as he grows he becomes increasingly adept at telling where his surroundings leave off and where he begins. He comes to see other people as external to him and gradually sees the connection between his effect on others and the gratification of his needs and desires. As he comes to recognize more and more such connections, the infant's inborn tendency to value all self-experience is replaced with a concern for how experiences are valued by those who play important roles in his life. This is the beginning of the infant's enculturation into society.

The enculturation process transforms the question "Do I like this?" into the question "Does someone important to me like this?" At the most basic level, Rogers views this process as instilling a conditional acceptance of natural experience, so that self-regard becomes dependent upon receiving personal regard from others. When self-gratifying actions overlap with actions that earn personal regard, the value the infant attaches to his experience is likely to be relatively independent of external acceptance. But when his spontaneous inclinations conflict with the way such activities are valued by others, the infant is susceptible to acquiring another's valuing system as if it were his own. Note, however, that while the *attitudes* an infant attaches to his experience can be shaped, the *feelings* evoked while having that experience can't. For instance, an infant can be conditioned to attach negative connotations to masturbating and, when he's old enough, can be conditioned to feel badly about himself for doing it. But he can't be convinced that masturbating doesn't feel good. Thus, the infant's feelings provide him with a reliable link to his unsocialized, unadapted self.

Whenever an individual substitutes personal regard from others for self-regard, he is susceptible to socialization. He is particularly susceptible when his security and satisfactions depend on the people, and later the social institutions, involved. The socialization will be incomplete, however, unless the individual learns how to protect himself against the feelings of anxiety evoked when he rejects his experience and goes against self-values. This requires a screening device that takes the form of defense mechanisms.

But the human being is infinitely complex, impulsive, and resourceful. Short of society providing a full-time shaper, as some who distrust man's benevolent impulses and natural tendencies have contended it should, the infant grows up partially unique, partially free, and partially able to value his own experience. Most important, Rogers claims, human beings can transcend earlier dependencies and perceptual distortions, and become increasingly independent and expansive in their thinking. New experiences, if received nondefensively, can reverse earlier conditioning. For example, there will come a time when people whom the child doesn't particularly care about try to control him. In such instances, the anxiety from not accurately representing his experience will outweigh the anxiety from not winning the support of these not-so-important others. The child will fight to accurately represent his experience and in the process will learn some things about self-determination.

As the child displays his capacity to be influenced by important others, these others begin to trust him more and relax the rate and extent to which they require that his pictures of reality match the ones they present him. After all, the key to having someone under control is knowing that the button exists and where it is, not in pushing it. In fact, there are experiments that demonstrate that conditioning proceeds most thoroughly when the desired behavior is rewarded, and the non-desired behavior is punished intermittently, rather than every time. Intermittant reinforcement causes the child to act in the desired way on his own because he can't predict exactly which event will bring a response from his shaper. In the process, the child gets taken in by the illusion that he is acting of his own volition. This illusion is important to the self-concept of the shaper as well as the child. Few people like to see themselves either excessively controlling someone else or being excessively controlled.

By the time we become adults in organizations, we're well practiced in substituting acceptance by others for acceptance that comes directly from our own experience. We automatically reflect, "What's the appropriate thing to say?" "What am I expected to feel?" In seeking constantly to avoid feelings of deviancy, we blind ourselves to self-affirming questions like, "What do *I* think?" "What do *I* want to do?" "What do *I* feel?" Our concern with acceptance so intimidates us that we're blocked from questioning the culture that censors our expression and that gets us, often by our silence, to censor anyone who dares to break from convention.

By the time we become established members of an organization, our needs for external affirmation are so pervasive and intense that it becomes difficult, if not impossible, for us to see how the organization's procedures and structure play on this need. We become so concerned with whether or not we are getting other people's approval that we fail to question whether the behavior that evokes their approval has intrinsic value to us. We say what the other person expects to hear, rather than express ourselves candidly; we create good impressions, follow protocol, dress acceptably, perform according to role, and so on. At almost every opportunity, our omnipresent need for external affirmation leads us to seek acceptance from just about every animate object. We don't even need much contact with people. We can imagine a conversation that never takes place or attribute to someone feelings that we have never tested.

We frequently compromise our values and judgments if people then approve of us. Meet someone new, perhaps at a cocktail party, and discuss something as trivial as a movie. We say, "I really had a good time with that film." He replies, "I thought the plot was bad and the acting was shallow." We're quick to hedge and say something like, "I guess I just needed an escape film that day."

We're always, it seems, working hard to find our commonalities with others, to give others an opportunity to agree with us (and in the process, affirm our own point of view). We gratuitously agree with someone else and then derive self-affirmation from the fact that, in our minds, this person sees us as sufficiently important to reinforce his point of view. Not only does all this keep us from developing better realities, but, by ignoring the feelings attached to our experience, we lose what little connection we have to our unadapted natures.

Reflection

Our situation is analogous to the effects of sugar and sacharin in rat experiments. Rats drinking a saccharin solution remain hungry, and rats drinking a sugar solution become satiated. In both instances, rats drink because they are hungry; but in one case, they're getting caloric value and can stop. Similarly, external affirmation without real self-valuing does not nourish us and help us grow, while self-regard does. Of course, there are many times when external valuing is consonant with self-experience and thus proves nourishing. But when we accept affirmation for an inauthentic expression, we no sooner get · affirmed than we need another fix.

CHAPTER 9

How the Organization Exploits Our Need for Acceptance

Our needs for external affirmation are so great that we are willing to subordinate our independently based pictures of reality to the prevailing view of the system. Because we would rather reject our own experience than risk being denied this acceptance, we are highly vulnerable to exploitation by the organization system. The effects of such exploitation can be seen in any number of work practices that impose artificial limitations on our personal styles. They are seen in the moral judgments we impose on ourselves and heap upon others, in the ways work problems get defined and dealt with, and in the paternalistic practices we accept as characterizing a benevolent management. Let's look at these practices in more detail to see what we're up against and what must be changed if we're to exert greater control over our organization life.

Moralistic Judgments

Our dependence on external affirmation leads us to judge ourselves and others against standards which are not really ours. The values of the organization system become our own. In fact, these values become implanted in our minds as if they constituted a moral code that we must observe. We worship competence, results, and dedication to the job. We seldom tell someone above us in the hierarchy that what he wants can wait, is not all that important, or isn't worth the pressure it creates. We attend meetings religiously, even when we know in advance that we'll be bored. In our efforts to meet organization standards, we are unable to act on values that are truly our own.

As with any moral code, there are violations. But because our beliefs result from conditioning, we cling to them more rigidly than we would if they came directly from experience. When their validity is questioned, we get defensive precisely because we have no rationale to support our position. The effect is similar to one of those experiments where a subject is hypnotized into voicing an attitude that's inconsistent with all the other things he believes. When he is awakened and these inconsistencies are brought out into the open, he will get defensive, and stretch and distort common logic in order to make incompatible assumptions fit with one another. We see similar distorted logic at work when we take home empty briefcases lest someone get the impression that we've stopped taking our job seriously.

The rigidity with which we hold organizationally imposed standards makes it difficult for us to analyze a violation without getting emotional. Violations feel like moral transgressions. When we're the violator, we feel guilty. We confess to crimes we didn't commit just to get past the punishment. We prefer to agree, "Yes, I made a mistake by not going through channels," rather than argue whether going through channels was necessary in the first place. When someone else is the violator, we allow ourselves to get righteous about actions in which we ourselves indulge. We criticize a colleague for knocking off early for a round of golf or for fooling around with Miss Whatshername with the great knees. Yet we are likely to feel puzzled by the intensity of the emotion we display. How often has a co-worker suddenly become very serious after we've said something flip like "I'm only in this job for the money." And then, much to our surprise, we find ourselves saluting every standard of commitment and allegiance to the organization as if we had said something for which we needed to atone.

The tendency to levy moral judgments is a prime contributor to the almost constant stream of criticism, backbiting, put downs, and negative judgments one hears around some organizations. Everyone tries to avoid guilt and censure by blaming others for ineffective performances and human acts that violate organization standards. For instance, there's the boss who says, "The trouble with Ed is that he never comes to me with his half-baked ideas." And Ed says, "My boss always appears too busy for me to raise the philosophical questions we need to discuss." Inevitably, our judgments prove to be little more than uninformed interpretations about why others act the way they do. Like Ed and his boss, we shall continue to blame and bypass one another until we sit down and openly contrast our individual pictures of what's going on.

When someone acts differently than we think he should, we seldom have an accurate understanding of what's happening; yet we're often critical of his motivations or abilities. We see this in the district manager who is constantly criticized behind his back for not being human with the people working for him. Because he's so technically competent, it never occurs to anyone that he's actually quite shy and doesn't know how to make social conversation with people. We see this in the animosity we direct toward the guy who spends the day making personal telephone calls, until we find out that he's in the throes of marital difficulties.

It's so easy to discover someone else's frame of reference; we merely have to ask him. But, instead, we turn part of our organization life into a combat zone by judging others before the facts are in. We immediately react with anger when someone misses an important meeting or makes an independent decision on which we feel we should have been consulted. Not only do we fail to take into account conditions that might justify such deviations but we refuse to consider whether or not the organization might be better off if our expectations were challenged more often.

By continuing in our moralistic ways, we defend and perpetuate actions that interfere with our real effectiveness. Our moral judgments create tensions between us and the very people we need to help us change unsuitable procedures. We are involved in a terrible irony here: although we are the ones who have the most to gain by the organization system becoming less moralistic, we are the ones who keep things going the way they are.

Problem-solving Styles

Our need for external affirmation excessively influences how we define and solve problems. Thus, in large organizations, it's commonplace for problems to be defined at one organization level and solved by people at the next lower level. This results in people at each successive lower level receiving a narrower definition of a problem than the people above them. Take the hospital administrator who is concerned about the lack of responsibility shown by the staff for the overall operation of the hospital. He focuses on the problem of phones that aren't being answered during the lunch hour. Then the supervisor to whom he complained installed a time clock to make sure the schedule for lunch breaks worked. Thus, we wind up basing our solutions on parameters set down by a "problem identifier." Perhaps a supervisor with a different boss would find a less coercive means for insuring telephone coverage and improving people's identification with the running of the hospital.

As a general rule, the people identifying a problem have more organization power than the people assigned to solve it. And while the problem identifier is almost always formally charged with evaluating the problem solver's work, only rarely does a problem solver evaluate the person telling him what to do. Lacking such parity in evaluation, the problem solver has little recourse but to do the job he thinks has been defined for him, which usually means suppressing some of his own ideas. This helps explain why people who have been highly successful on previous assignments often muff their first assignment for a new boss.

Not only do problem solvers lack the power to help define the problems and tasks but their problem-solving mandate doesn't demand that they come up with the best possible solution. In the first place, most organization problems are little more than someone's arbitrary decision that something needs to be done. In the same situation, different people will see different problems. For instance, the problem faced by the new recruits who never met with the plant manager could be termed the recruits' hang-up with authority, their immediate supervisors' inability to manage, or the system's overreliance on hierarchy. Because there is no statement of the problem everyone would agree with what needs to be done is usually a particular person's idea of what will put order in a turbulent organization world.

Second, when problems are arbitrarily defined, it's hard to tell the best answer from an adequate one. For instance, what do we say when the company president asks us how we can best meet community demands for corporate responsibility? We tell him what makes sense for him, not necessarily for the community. In trying to put order into someone else's unique picture of the world, we're very dependent on which criteria *he* feels need to be met.

Third, the types of problems people work on these days are usually so complex that it is difficult to envision how a solution will stack up against all the criteria on which it is being assessed. Consider, for example, the dilemmas faced by the personnel man who was asked to prepare a report on the best way for his company to staff its new overseas operations. He had to examine everything from national politics to the fatigue factors of overseas travel.

Thus, in most organizations, our problem-solving techniques are ultimately judged according to whether or not we follow the methods and procedures that our evaluators are convinced will lead to a proper solution. In order to get a good rating, it's usually more important to show that we took the required steps than to come up with the best result possible. We go through *all* the steps and just-in-case procedures so that we can justify our position when problems arise. (Indeed, we learn to tell people how we've gone about solving the problem before we give them the answer.) Thus, we can get good grades for questionable solutions like the following classic memo: "We're going to have a meeting to discuss duplication in the department. It will be held Tuesday afternoon at one, two, three, and four." Such problem solving also allows us to promise solutions to problems that don't even exist. One manager told me, "I'm willing to guarantee anything with a time limit beyond six months because I know they'll change their minds before then."

In effect, the way to work successfully on a problem that somebody else has presented to us is to identify the assumptions that that person is making about which methods will lead to a good solution. Because our problem identifier is a problem solver for someone else higher up, we can expect that in time everyone in the organization is going to become enculturated with a similar set of assumptions. To the extent that we're not conscious of the discrepancies between our experience and the problem-solving style preferred by the system, we're vulnerable to taking on the organization's style as if it were our own.

It's problem-solving conditions like these that cause us to become more absorbed with issues of "What do I need to do to be successful?" than with issues of "What do I know that will produce a successful solution?" We rely on external acceptance at the expense of the self-acceptance we might gain from drawing more fully on our own expertise and experience. We might reason, though, that doing what other people want can also result in our being successful, which is what *we* want. When someone thinks like this, he's a tough person to argue with, because he fails to see the traps inherent in bypassing his own experience.

Of course, the above is somewhat exaggerated. Each of us has had the experience of trying to persuade someone who has given us an assignment that "This doesn't make sense!" But how many times will he answer us before he's even heard our reasons out? Even if he does listen, how often does he pass the buck by confiding that, although he agrees with us, this is the way the boss wants it? And because his boss is at least two steps above us in the hierarchy, we agree. Only afterward does it occur to us that if we're confronting him, and he's our boss, then why can't he confront his boss?

The range of problems a person is allowed to formulate and solve is also limited by his position in the hierarchy. For instance, I know any number of large corporations where first-level personnel are given latitude in the way they work on a project but not in choosing which project they work on; low-level managers are given latitude in who they assign to a project, but not on which projects need to be accomplished; middle-level managers are given latitude in determining which projects best direct organization resources toward established goals, but do not have much voice in determining what the goals ought to be; while upper-level managers reserve the right to determine organization policies and declare which goals best achieve these policies.

Notwithstanding these various constraints, all organization workers are allowed some areas where they're permitted to define problems. However, the way a person formulates a problem is usually biased to require his unique and special talents for solving it. Thus, a manager with expertise for shuffling people and work loads might respond to numerous client complaints by seeing the main problem as a mismatch between people and jobs. Another manager will respond to the same client complaints by focusing on problems in team coordination and communications. Coincidentally, he just happens to be an expert in using group techniques that improve communications and assist members in redesigning organization procedures.

In some ways, having an area where we can define the problem is as good for the organization as it is for us. The organization gets its job done expertly, and we get the chance to exercise authority. But there are also drawbacks. Because we are constantly on our guard against the jurisdictional challenges of others, we define power as our ability to get others to accept our definition of the problem. Yet if we were really in control, we might modify our definition of power to include the personal power that allows us to accept new ways of defining problems, especially in areas where we have ultimate authority. Concern over how to keep others out of our territory would then be replaced with concern over how to include others and incorporate valid suggestions.

Paternalistic Practices

Our needs for external affirmation keep us from demanding the information and perspectives we need in order to manage our organization life intelligently. Instead of finding out for ourselves what is going on in the organization and how we are seen, we allow others who claim to have this information, usually our bosses, to make it available to us as they see fit. However, their unconscious needs to keep us under control stop them from giving us this information directly. Instead, they leak it to us in a form that accentuates their benevolence and our dependency.

Management gives us some facts, but seldom enough for us to make our own decisions. This puts them in the parent's role of advising us what to do, and it places us in the child's role of trying to guess what they're implying we ought to do. Of course, everyone involved is sufficiently ambivalent to keep the situation from becoming too blatant. We say something like, "I'd like to get your thoughts on the matter, although I know it's my decision to make" and they respond, "I don't know anything for certain, all I can tell you is what I would do in your situation." This type of paternalism pervades today's organization system and strangely enough, is positively received by most of the people controlled by it. Indeed, such fatherly advice becomes proof of management's concern and interest in us as people.

This kind of paternalistic practice begins either when someone with information gives us unsolicited advice or makes decisions for us, or when we feel out of control and take comfort in believing that someone who is benevolent and powerful will watch out for us. It's shown when the department head tells us "Just in case you haven't read all the signals, the task force you've been asked to volunteer for is being closely watched by top management," but then refuses to give us more details.

A paternalistic pact is made when people with complementary assumptions— "I know what's good for you" and "He can help me"— find one another. When the person with the superior perspective also occupies a position of greater organization power, the paternalistic pact expands to include his offering of privileges, or rights, that we don't feel we could take without the sanction of someone with more authority. Thus, we drag ourselves into the office hoping that our boss will notice and say, "You look beat. Why not take a day of compensatory leave to make up for all the traveling you've been doing."

Paternalistic advice carries with it the implicit message that, if only we had a better perspective on ourselves and the organization, we would make the same decisions, follow the prescribed action, or be entitled to the same privileges. But the authority of the person who gives it implies that the limits of time, organizational confidentiality, and our lack of self-objectivity make it difficult for him to tell us the facts and, thus, put his superior perspective to the test.

Paternalism induces feelings of dependency, passivity, and helplessness in us. Probably because most of us didn't get enough benevolent fathering when we were children, we seem to linger with the dream that some day someone whom we can trust will come along with a better perspective on our life than we can provide for ourselves. We are setups for anyone whose actions imply that he's authoritative and knowledgeable. We see him as the *mavin*, the expert whose advice we should follow. And we know better. We know this person lacks information about crucial aspects of our life without which he can't possibly be smarter than we are about ourselves.

In the short run, an organization where this type of paternalism is widespread will enjoy a number of benefits. Its management can expect obedience, predictability, and coordination. However, over the longer run, this order is accomplished at the expense of our assertiveness, autonomy, risk-taking, and complexity. Paternalistic practices give rise to a sort of self-fulfilling prophecy whereby we are dependent on the advice of management and management interprets our dependence as a request for more direction. They then make more decisions and take additional action on our behalf. But by withholding the information on which their decisions are based, they leave us feeling even less on top of things and more in need of managerial counsel than before.

Reflection

In this chapter, we have considered some of the ways in which the organization system, as we live it, exploits our dependence on external affirmation. We will eliminate much of the seaminess of organization life once we learn to form pictures of reality without constraining what we see by what we think will be acceptable.

Each of us seeks a life-style and benefits that are only possible when we pool our efforts within some type of organization system. A greater degree of self-acceptance and independence would allow for a more open-ended examination of some crucial questions, such as, "What alternative ways of organizing involve fewer—and less critical—compromises than we're currently making?" and "What goals should we abandon and what should we replace them with in our quest to live a self-fulfilling organization life?"

While these questions are fairly practical, they are also existential. All of us will spend a major portion of our lives trying to bring about the resolutions we have reached today. Ultimately, we will settle for the life we lead. However, there are some things we can do to further enrich our lives before we accept what we have achieved, and these will occur to us as we develop greater skills in learning the tacit lessons contained in our experience. The next part is intended as a guide to you to do just that.

PART III

Getting Out
of the Traps

CHAPTER 10

A General Strategy for Getting Out of Traps

> It is only the oppressed who, by freeing themselves,
> can free the oppressors.
>
> Paulo Freire

It is up to us to make organization life more human. This requires learning how to explicate the tacit lessons contained in our experience and transforming these lessons into organization improvements. The learning process is deeply personal, while changing the system involves the rest of humanity and is thus universal. Connecting our needs with the organization's needs can produce an exhilaration that both radicalizes us and humanizes us. In areas where we are oppressed, we see how we can develop new and better possibilities, and in areas where we oppress others, we see the wisdom of working with them to set things straight.

Consciousness-raising can be an awesome, time-consuming, emotionally volatile, and disorienting process. It is continual in that goals are never met completely and rewards are often not apparent. A road map is necessary to maintain our direction and to comprehend what we've accomplished. Such a road map often takes the form of a *model* that relates what is presently occurring to the overall scheme of events. Without some structure, we get lost.

The remainder of this book explicates one model that gives structure and focus to our consciousness-raising activities. This model was evolved in the process of trying to help technical staff and managers of various organization levels learn the lessons of their experience and avoid the cultural traps written about by Vickers, Freire, Marcuse, and others. Of course, there are traps in any strategy that offers a road map to freedom, and, from one standpoint, that is exactly the type of model I'm about to offer. No doubt, the model I'm presenting here will eventually need to be discarded. My hope, however, is that it will at least help you to recognize its replacement.

The Model

The model portrays a strategy for gaining greater control of our organization life, a strategy that entails a process of consciousness-raising and self-directed resocialization. In theory, this process can be broken down into five sequential stages, each of which involves a separate consciousness-raising activity. In practice, of course, these five stages can be intermingled and used out of sequence. Where possible, however, the stages should be followed in sequence because the insights developed at one stage provide the beginning points for consciousness-raising at the next stage. Learning at each stage depends on our developing skills and receiving peer group support.

Consciousness-raising can best be accomplished by focusing on a single area of organization concerns and working our way through each of the five stages of the model. Maintaining focus on a single area at a time requires discipline because insights in one area inevitably spark insights in others. Overall, the consciousness-raising process can be likened to eating an artichoke. One starts with the less meaty leaves on the periphery and progressively spirals in toward the more meaty leaves closer to the heart. Unlike eating an artichoke, however, we don't reach the heart, that is, gain control over our organization life; we merely get closer. Each insight paves the way for a meatier realization.

Experience in using this model has shown that a preliminary overview of all five stages facilitates a deeper understanding of each stage. That is the purpose of this chapter. Subsequent chapters will alternate between descriptions of the actions needed to progress through each stage and guidelines for working with a group of similarly situated people to put these actions into practice. The chapters dealing with actions will contain in-depth illustrations of people encountering the opportunities available at that stage of consciousness-raising.

STAGE 1: Recognizing What's "Off"

Consciousness-raising begins with a gut experience. We develop a vague awareness that something in our organization life is "off," although we can't quite put our fingers on exactly what it is. Such feelings of incoherence are frequent occurrences in our organization life, but usually we try to forget about them. However, if we want our consciousness raised, we've got to be ready to pay attention to what seems minor. Closer scrutiny will usually show much more beneath the surface than we saw originally.

Our vague feelings of incoherence serve as clues to identifying discrepancies between our nature and the expectations of the organization system. Such discrepancies usually fall into one of two categories. The first is when the organization seems to expect something that is unnatural for us or inconsistent with our best interests. The second is when we do what comes naturally and learn afterward that it was deemed inappropriate by the system.

Transforming feelings of incoherence into a more precise statement of discrepancies requires some concepts and some emotional support. The concepts will help us pinpoint where we and the organization are in conflict, and the support will help us resist our tendency to shoulder all the blame for these conflicts.

STAGE 2: Understanding Ourselves and the Organization

Being able to specify discrepancies may make us feel that we can now proceed to solve our problems with the organization and put our minds at ease. Usually, this proves to be a short-sighted strategy. We need to treat discrepancies for what they are, symptoms rather than problems. In practice, taking our conflicts with the organization at face value and "resolving" them can be the surest way to keep from seeing the fundamental ills of the system as we currently live it.

Treating discrepancies as symptoms, on the other hand, helps us to understand aspects of ourselves and the organization that we had not previously recognized. We have a chance to probe beneath the discrepancy by asking ourselves what human qualities and what organization attributes can produce the conflicts we're experiencing.

Transforming discrepancies into new understanding requires skills to think divergently and support to resist our inclinations to think convergently. Divergent thinking keeps us focused on the fact that a discrepancy is a symptom of some lack in basic understanding. The support we get will help us resist our impulses to converge on a solution that prematurely puts our anxieties to rest.

STAGE 3: Understanding Our Relationship
with the Organization

Greater understanding of ourselves and of the organization system helps us to recognize alternatives that suit our interests and to resist external attempts to control us. We sense a new personal freedom. However, getting carried away by this "freedom" proves to be another short-term strategy for gaining control. It puts us underground, "working" the system. But eventually, those who however unwittingly influence and control us will discover that we've eluded them, and we'll be back playing cat and dog again.

In order to really improve things, we'll need, at some point, to focus directly on our relationship with the organization. The new understanding we developed in Stage 2, about ourselves and the organization, can now be transformed into a more thorough understanding of the assumptions that link us to the organization system. This requires that we learn about our conditioning in the organization and that we get assistance in doing this from people we trust. Some of our biases are so ingrained we will require tough-minded challenging to break through to them.

STAGE 4: Moving toward a More Natural Life
in the Organization

Increased understanding of ourselves, the organization, and our relationship with the organization will give us a new sense of power; we can now formulate the types of relationships that will give us greater control over our organization life. But while we can envision more optimal relationships, we do not yet know all that we need to know in order to see whether we can formulate alternatives that express our self-interests and yet appear practical from the standpoint of organization goals.

Transforming understanding of ourselves, the organization, and the assumptions that link us to the organization into practical alternatives also requires new skills and support. We need skills in identifying tensions between assumptions the organization makes about us and the person we're discovering ourselves to be. We need support to help us reflect on personal priorities before getting caught up in our attempts to renegotiate our relationship with the organization.

STAGE 5: Affecting the Organization
Lives of Others

Being able to envision practical alternatives gives us a great deal of control over our organization life. We derive a new sense of independence from knowing that our options are no longer limited to the best ideas that others have for us. However, as long as others in the organization are still out of control, their spontaneous actions will set off forces that oppose the mutually beneficial directions we may try to take.

Making suggestions that change and improve the organization system requires that we be mindful of the personal realities of all the people affected. To adopt a strategy where we impose our improvements on others runs counter to our reasons for wanting change in the first place. We need to think about change as if we were statesmen concerned with the well-being of all the people. We need support from a peer group that recognizes what we're trying to accomplish and that can help us maintain our focus at times when it's difficult for us to observe the effects our efforts are having.

Reflection

This model is applicable to most nontechnical aspects of organization life. It is one attempt to reverse the machinery of a run-away system that influences us without our knowing it.

Gaining control eventually means probing all critical areas of organization life. However, the best place to start is with the area that is currently causing the greatest discomfort. This is where you've got the energy to maintain your focus. Of course, the first area will require the greatest concentration because you'll not only be learning specific things about your organization life but you'll also be acquiring the analytic skills necessary for consciousness-raising. Thus, you can expect a cumulative effect that enables gains made in one area to shorten the work needed in another. Nevertheless, consciousness-raising is a continuing process that requires returning over and over again to the same areas.

CHAPTER 11

Stage 1: Recognizing What's "Off"

Often in our organization life we think that we're on top of things while actually we have little idea of what's happening to us or what we're doing to others. We fail to see where our practice is less than ideal, and where our actual working conditions are different from what we've been led to expect. If we could identify such discrepancies, we'd have the beginnings of the perspective we need to put our relationship with the system on a more realistic basis. Let me illustrate with an example.

Example

In the academic system at UCLA, where I work, people are constantly being caught in the discrepancy between their belief that the publish-or-perish meat grinder has been done away with and the reality of what is actually going on. Some time ago, our administration formally acknowledged that a variety of professorial duties went into building a quality university and that different people might have different types of excellence to contribute; that is, that some might be outstanding teachers and administrators who do not necessarily excel at research, while others might be excellent researchers who do not necessarily make outstanding teachers or administrators. The administration further acknowledged that people go through different phases during which teaching, administration, or research may be more central to their careers.

In this way, university administrators hoped to convince the students that the quality of teaching was evaluated and rewarded, and the professors that committee work and other administrative assignments counted. This was necessary because if the students stopped believing that teaching mattered, or if the faculty realized that teaching and administration had only a marginal influence on their promotions, the system might temporarily break down. But only temporarily, because if such a discrepancy arose, the students would demand some way of insuring teaching excellence, and the faculty would refuse to spend extra hours doing quality committee work until they were duly rewarded. But had the publish-or-perish ethic really changed?

Recently, a colleague named Tom was denied tenure because his research wasn't up to par. Usually, refusal of tenure is tantamount to being fired. But, in this instance, Tom had an outstanding record of teaching and committee service, and firing him would have created an obvious discrepancy between the administration's professed and actual criteria in making promotion decisions. It would have led the students to realize that their participation in course evaluations didn't really count and the faculty to realize that the long hours they spend pitching in on administrative work wasn't going to do much for their careers. At another level, Tom's dismissal would have caused university administrators to feel guilty as they came to realize that in the process of trying to make their ideal system work, they had misled Tom.

University administrators are like the rest of us, consciously we want to be equal to our ideals, but unconsciously we want it both ways if we can get it. In order to maintain the illusion that other activities besides research truly mattered, while at the same time keeping other professors focused on doing research, an illusionary mechanism needed to be found. They found one. The administration decided to release Tom from all duties other than research and to consider him for promotion again the following year.

On the surface, it seemed as if Tom was getting the opportunity he needed to prove himself. The administrators, the students, the faculty, even Tom himself, were all delighted that Tom was getting this chance. However, at the unconscious level, this decision helped the members of the system to avoid seeing what kind of productivity truly counts.

Thus, the administration's solution was subversive, no matter from whose perspective it is viewed. For Tom, it was subversive because it had the effect of systematically stripping him of all those tasks in which he had succeeded, locking him up in his office to come eyeball to eyeball with his failures. Tom's research area is close to my own, and it requires time in the field to see what's going on before sitting down and writing theoretically. But the pressure was on him to write.

Firing Tom, on the other hand, would have allowed him to leave feeling good about his teaching and administrative skills, although perhaps bitter about being misled by the system. But if he were to fail to get promoted the following year, he'd be likely to leave without feeling good about his areas of established excellence.

The action was also subversive for the faculty because they could see that Tom's dedication was being rewarded with extra privileges and could thus continue to believe that teaching and committee work really counted. It was subversive for the students because they could continue to believe that their anonymous end-of-term evaluations of faculty mattered. Finally, the action had a subversive effect on the administrators because the year's delay in their probable firing of Tom gave them a way to avoid facing up to how their system actually operated. They would probably feel okay about firing him the next year when they could think, "We gave him every chance, and there's no reason for us to feel guilty."

Feelings of Incoherence and Discrepancies

We are seldom out of control for a long time without experiencing internal signals, however vague, that something is off. I call these signals *feelings of incoherence*. Basically, there are two kinds of conflicts, or *discrepancies*, that produce such feelings of incoherence. The first is produced when the system expects something unnatural to us or inconsistent with our best interests. For Tom, these feelings would be produced if he were to accept the system's assumption that the only factor stopping him from publishing enough research to be promoted was insufficient time to write. The second type of discrepancy is produced when we do what seems to come naturally only to discover afterward that what we did was disapproved of, inappropriate, or wrong. For Tom, such feelings might come were he to undervalue his accomplishments in teaching and school service because they weren't sufficient to get him promoted.

By and large, feelings of incoherence tend to be ignored. This is not

72

because they are so very uncomfortable. They're not. But acknowledging their presence sends us on a search for discrepancies in our relationship with the system. Facing up to such discrepancies is unpleasant, even painful, because we're conditioned to think, "If something is off, it's off with me, not the system." This is our continuing problem with self-acceptance. If we were capable of more self-regard and were less dependent on personal regard from others, we wouldn't resist facing up to discrepancies nearly as much as we do.

Instead of acknowledging incoherences and tracking down the discrepancies they signal, we do different things to avoid them. We avoid the pain of the first type of discrepancy, in which the system expects something unnatural from us, by going along with their demands and pretending not to notice that we're doing something inconsistent with our nature. In the example, Tom could protect himself from pain in the short run by obediently marching off to his office to write, reasoning that he finally has the time to do the writing he'd wanted to do all along.

We avoid the pain of the second type of discrepancy, in which we learn that doing what came naturally creates problems, by rejecting our own perspectives, and internalizing the norms and expectations of the system as if they were our own. For many of my colleagues in academia, this means publishing two or three articles a year without much personal concern for their actual relevance. The consequences of both these defenses is the same: we subordinate our pictures of reality to those of the system and thereby choose self-alienation over external rejection.

But we're never quite successful in numbing ourselves to the feelings of incoherence that signal the presence of discrepancies in our relationship with the system. When you see someone popping tranquilizers on the job, there's a good chance that he's trying to get himself past the feelings that are provoked when a discrepancy grows too large for him to dismiss.

Feelings of incoherence, which are clues to consciousness, could be used better if we had support to resist our conditioned inclination to attribute their cause to personal shortcomings. If we had sufficient support to examine incoherences on an objective, nonemotional level, we'd have access to the information we need to raise our consciousness and set straight those who are influential in making the system work the way it does.

Support

Support comes in many forms. It can come in the form of structure— for example, job security for teachers or negotiated rights for union workers. Such support gives people dependable guidelines for speaking their minds or demanding certain rights. Support may come in the form of close interpersonal relationships—for example, the trust developed in a group of friends or colleagues working for the same organization. Such support allows people to discuss personal issues that might be used against them if divulged outside the group. Support may come in the form of group identities—for example, the norms and sanctions shared in groups like Weight Watchers or Alcoholics Anonymous. Such support gives people the rituality they need to achieve some desired standard. Support may come in the form of people with like needs attempting to develop certain skills. Master-apprentice relationships and encounter groups for increasing interpersonal skills are good examples. Such support gives group members a sense of common purpose, which motivates them to be helpful to one another. Any or all of these types of support may be helpful to us when we attempt to clarify and change our relationship to an organization system.

Our ability to face these conflicts depends on the support we get. We often overlook just how much support we do need. Facing up to unresolved tensions that we have lived with for years makes us anxious. Conceptualizing the causes of these tensions, without blaming ourselves, requires some ego bolstering. As one manager said, "My boss puts a lot of energy into my believing that I'm worthless if I have problems with my job, and now you come along and want me to confess to problems that neither higher management nor I know about." Without support, we feel like one poor bastard pitted against all the problems of the world; with it, we're one of many involved in a very human dilemma.

One person alone cannot stand the anxiety of raised consciousness. You may think that some do, but show me someone who has a substantially better picture of organizational reality than his co-workers, and I'll show you a man with a hidden support system, perhaps even a psychotherapist, or a man who has consciousness but little idea of what constructive actions to take with it. The latter is usually labeled a cynic, which allows others in the organization to dismiss his views as unnecessarily negative. The cynic is so uptight about being taken in by someone's poorly thought out perspectives that it's difficult to get him to commit to a course of action, even one consistent with his experience. The positive thinker, on the other hand, is both the enemy and the hero of my model. He's the enemy because his basic orientation is to distort the world until it is closer to his ideals, which, of course, is exactly what screws things up for the rest of us. He's the hero because once he sees what's off, he's poised for constructive action.

A catharsis, dissipating the tension and anxiety produced by facing up to discrepancies, can occur when going through a consciousness-raising process with a group of people who are more or less in the same boat. In fact, it is crucial to do this with people who have comparable relationships to the organization. Discrepancies look different to people at different levels and with different roles, causing people at one level to feel that they're not given much chance to act creatively and their supervisors, considering the same aspect, to argue that lower levels of the organization just aren't very creative. Keep these groups separate, find some way to bolster self-esteem, and you may find people at both levels relatively open to, eventually coming up with, complementary conceptualizations. The lower-ranked group may reflect, "We joined this organization to work creatively, but now find ourselves rather dull." The supervisory group may reflect, "The organization needs creativity, but apparently we're not able to inspire much of it." Mix these groups together without first giving members a supportive setting for facing self-doubts, and these groups will most likely blame one another and generally act defensive. Engage a single individual alone in consciousness-raising on the topic of his role in organizational creativity, and it's tantamount to asking him to admit either that he's personally uncreative or that he's personally unable to inspire creativity in others.

But when a homogeneous group of people raises its consciousness about discrepancies in its relationships to an organization system the implications reach far beyond the specific discrepancies involved. Ultimately, such consciousness-raising is a radicalizing experience. The participants learn firsthand that different experiences produce different realities, and they see the traps in letting others, or precedent, define their experience. They also learn the inevitability of their having a blind side. They discover that one can never anticipate all the consequences his actions may pose for others and that good intentions do not insure consciousness.

An example of the importance in monitoring this blind side is seen in a continuation of the story of the professor who was denied tenure. When I asked the administrator who had come up with the idea of giving the professor an additional year to do his writing what he had had in mind, he replied that "Tom's a good man. It seems like we need to make sure we can keep him around." When I suggested that his action was unlikely to accomplish this because I did not see how Tom could produce in one year's time the type of writing that the evaluation committee would respect, he paled sufficiently to convince me that he was in fact sincere. "I guess," he confided, "I got so caught up in the beauty of the solution that I overlooked that at the time." I next asked him if he had experienced any funny feelings about this situation. He said, "Yes, of course I did, but I always feel funny about evaluation issues at our school, so I didn't make anything special out of Tom's case." I walked away from this experience with an even stronger realization that no one can be counted on to monitor his own realities correctly and that each of us needs people we trust to listen to our perspectives and point out additional ones.

Another effect of such consciousness-raising touches people's fears about fundamental change. I can best illustrate this by relating a conversation I had with a high-level manager. I was reflecting that a recent group discussion was really centering around painless ways to get rid of problems without making any fundamental changes in the ways group members operated. He said, "Listen, Sam, we don't do so badly around here. What makes you think that we could benefit from changing? In fact, I think things would even get worse if we made changes." This brought me up short. I reflected for a few moments and said, "It's not that I care so much whether or not you change anything. I merely want you to see what fundamentally different possibilities look like so that you have some choice." This conversation was clarifying for both of us. The manager saw that he was prematurely figuring out how to implement something radically different rather than simply reflecting on whether or not some new perspective might enrich his current way of seeing things. As for me, I realized that I didn't trust him to consider any different alternatives, so I sounded like I wanted change just for the sake of change.

Reflection

Facing discrepancies is only the first step in comprehending our situation in the organization. All we know are the conflicts. We've yet to discover what we need to know about ourselves and the organization in order to develop fundamental resolutions to the conflicts. Until we have a better perspective on ourselves and the organization, it's unlikely that any solutions that occur to us will have long-standing relevance. Chapter 13 will discuss the theory and resources needed to transform discrepancies into such understanding. But before we get into that, we need to consider some of the practical matters of developing sufficient support that helps us transform feelings of incoherence into explicated discrepancies. This is the subject of the next chapter.

CHAPTER 12

Getting Support from a Consciousness-raising Group

This chapter presents guidelines that a group of people with common concerns can use to form a support group. Of course, when it comes to people working together in groups, no guideline can be taken as an absolute. First, our understanding of group processes is incomplete, and second, there's no way of anticipating the chemistry developed when unique personalities, with various needs, with different backgrounds, and perhaps at different stages of life, come together. Moreover, no two groups of people will invent exactly the same projects, and each project requires its own special procedures. Thus, we've got to remember to be flexible with any guideline that a group decides to follow. On the assumption that you will make modifications in the support group as you see fit, here are my suggested ground rules for group composition, size, duration, leadership, process, style, and format.

Group Composition

Support groups should include only those people who have a similar relationship to a set of organization concerns which serves as the rallying point for the group's existence. Common experiences and concerns provide the support and energy for the group to do its work. If, for example, the rallying point is to be the tensions resulting from being a black manager in a predominantly white organization, then group energy is drained and support is lost by including managers who are white.

It's also desirable to protect the people involved from the full force of the competitive and political forces that exist among people who work together. Thus, it's best that support groups be composed of people who have similar relationships to an organization but whose actual work responsibilities do not regularly put them in direct competition with one another. For this reason, it's sometimes best to form groups with people having similar relationships to different organizations.

It's important for people to be able to participate freely, knowing that their personal feelings, struggles, and fears will not be used against them. If, for example, the issue sparking a support group's existence is the impact of business travel on family life, then it would be best to include both husbands and wives, *providing* that travel is viewed as a stress *between* families and the organization and not as something that husbands and wives use against one another when fighting about other issues. It would also be desirable for such a group to be composed of people who perceive themselves as having a similar amount of control over their travel schedules. At the same time, they should not be people working in the same department, if the unwillingness of one person to travel puts additional pressures on someone else in the group.

It's desirable that support groups include people who are more or less equal in organization rank. We can't reasonably expect someone of lesser rank to empathize with someone who controls and limits the freedom of people like himself, particularly when individual freedom is the underlying issue in consciousness-raising. Moreover, combining people of different organization ranks can raise expectations that those with higher ranks will perform as experts. Yet each person is his own best resource when it comes to recognizing feelings of incoherence, or to searching for discrepancies. The presence of people with different status may only confuse the issue.

Group Size

I recommend a group of between five and twenty, largely because these numbers represent the size range of consciousness-raising groups I've experienced and for which I can vouch. Perhaps, if I had been part of groups with memberships between four and twenty-one, I would have cited these numbers. The group of twenty contained both women and men, and I doubt that I would have enjoyed working with a group that large if it had been composed only of men. But group homogeneity is a relative concept, and there are always going to be differences. When there's an obvious subcategory I recommend that at least two of its members be included. For example, if women are to be included among a first-level manager grouping that is mostly men, I recommend including at least two women. Having 50 percent women is best. These considerations are more important as group size becomes larger, and less crucial, although still relevant, when the group is very small.

Group Duration

It is more important that all members of the group have a similar set of time expectations and commitments than how often or how long they meet. Thus, I recommend that group members begin with an agreement of from one to three meetings and then, toward the conclusion of the last meeting, evaluate progress and decide whether or not to contract for another set of meetings. I recommend that successive sets of meetings number not less than three nor more than five. Having the possible ending point come too frequently can disturb members' commitment to the group's progress. Having it delayed too long allows the group to go on longer than it should without monitoring its progress and the feelings of individual members. While it's not desirable for members to drop out during an agreed upon set of meetings (because it destroys a structure that gets people to give their true reactions to how the group is operating) it's important that each person be free to quit when he feels like it. Nor is it a good practice to add members once the group has gotten beyond its second or third meeting. Groups quickly develop their own cultures, and adding new members subjects them to socializing forces without the means to understand why they are expected to uphold certain patterns. For groups in which some members want to continue and others do not, I recommend that the group disband and a new group form, including at least half new recruits. Having as many as even 50 percent old members can get a little touchy if they bring with them set ideas of how things ought to be.

Group Leadership

I am categorically against any consciousness-raising group where the leader is perceived to be the expert. The reasoning here is similar to not wanting people of higher organization rank present: there should be nothing about the group that caters to our natural tendency to defer to authority. For example, I have been in groups where my expertise in group process was emphasized until people reacted to me as if I should know how they ought to be acting and thinking about themselves. Worse, I've seen myself succumb to this seduction. If a group process expert is asked to organize a consciousness-raising session, I think it's essential for him to get personally involved in the learning and, when contributing professionally, to do so as a consultant, not as a leader.

Once a group decides on a discussion format and on a style to support its members, it can agree upon a leadership role that insures these processes. After this has been decided, who carries out this function becomes less important than the mere fact that someone assumes coordinating responsibilities. Because coordination distracts a person from acting naturally in the group, I suggest that a new leader be selected at the beginning of each session. However, when the call for volunteers goes out, I also suggest picking the second, not the first, volunteer because members can use the role as a defense against participating openly; defenses can arise when we're most anxious and probably most needful of opening ourselves up to others.

Group Process

The structure and format of a support group depend upon the assumptions we make about what we're trying to accomplish and why we need others. Explicating these assumptions provides a theory that guides the group's process and allows us to experiment with format and consciousness-raising activities. We are thus able to monitor our progress and make adjustments as they are warranted.

A group begins its theory building with each member sharing personal experiences related to the underlying concern of the group. For instance, a group of managers discussing problems in supervising others might begin by relating stories that illustrate their frustrations.

Listening to the reports of others struggling with dilemmas comparable to our own imparts a great deal of implicit support. This support unleashes pent-up frustrations, even anger to the point of rage. Such release clears the air for more sober thinking. Eventually, we begin fantasizing aloud about changes that will improve things.

As each person reports his unique experience, we discover some common themes. We begin to see how our individual concerns fit within a broader set of concerns. This allows us to formulate a set of goals that we can use for working out our concerns within a group context. After we've discussed these with others and agreed on a set of group goals, we need to talk about the type of discussion process and meeting format that will allow us to help one another achieve these goals.

The progress a support group makes can be evaluated by assessing how far its members have gotten in accomplishing their individual goals. However, when evaluating progress, we also need to reflect our theory against our experience. Are our goals and our means for accomplishing them still valid? Focusing only on whether or not we've accomplished anything keeps us absorbed in measuring improvement, and inhibits us from thinking about the personal validity of the directions on which we're proceeding.

There is at least one type of process from which a support group ought to refrain. This occurs when a number of people come together to raise the consciousness of but one member. I've been in too many situations like this, both in the roles of helper and helped, and know firsthand that this type of assistance carries a high price. Don't get me wrong, I'm not inferring that you shouldn't consult with friends about some organization problem that's bothering you. But, for example, if I were to gather together three to five colleagues and Tom, the professor who didn't get promoted, with the stated goal of raising each of our consciousnesses about the academic system, I'd bet Tom would feel stigmatized and put down. While the rest of us were talking more or less hypothetically about what we're likely to do in the future, Tom would be up to his ears in the present. While we could afford to carry on somewhat cavalierly because we were succeeding in the system, Tom would be motivated by fear; and our discussion would probably proceed at a faster pace than Tom would naturally go, given his current degree of threat and insecurity.

The overriding goal of this first stage of consciousness-raising involves dealing with feelings of incoherence and using them to identify discrepancies. Talking about incoherences requires a discussion style that circumvents the self-critical tendencies that hamper our objective assessment of discrepancies.

Discussion Style To Circumvent Self-Criticism

Hitting upon a discussion style that puts individual members at ease about *their* role in a discrepancy is the most difficult part of consciousness-raising. Most minority groups have overcompensated on this issue; too often consciousness-raising results in their blaming the system for all their conflicts. Many cannot get beyond their anger to a point where they can take constructive action. We see the same sort of thing in the early stages of the women's movement in the United States, when men were viewed as the enemy. It was not until women realized that the system was equally oppressive for men that they were able to make progress in coping with their culturally conditioned feelings of inadequacy.

There is no quick way to build the type of self-esteem that allows us to circumvent self-critical tendencies. Ultimately, each of us has something unique and deep to work out for himself. But within a support group, self-criticism can be, at least temporarily, sidestepped. After a period of catharsis, we can find ways of viewing problems so that we can get out from under self-critical tendencies and away from blaming the system. We can learn how to explicate discrepancies in relatively factual, nonjudgmental terms. No longer taking all the blame helps us develop better feelings about ourselves, and learning not to put down the system increases our self-valuing all the more.

In helping support group members circumvent their tendencies to be self-critical, I ask them to consider their problems as contingent with certain aspects of the system. While each of us has many prominent traits by which we can characterize ourselves, not one of these traits is applicable under all circumstances. We are not aggressive all the time, nor impulsive all the time, nor intelligent all the time. I suggest we replace such stereotypes by learning the conditions that lead us to act a certain way. If we're aggressive, we need to understand the conditions under which we are passive; if we're impulsive, we need to understand the conditions under which we are thoughtful. Similarly, in raising our consciousness about discrepancies in our relationships with organization systems, it's important to remember that there's an interaction between our behavior and the conditions present in the organization. Thus, theoretically speaking, we don't need to hold ourselves or the system totally to blame when we discover organization policies that treat us as if we were untrustworthy or when we realize that we create problems for others when we try to beat the system. With the help of support group members, you can find out that you're not the only one who turns in an expense statement for a first-class fare when you fly coach and take your spouse along.

Easier said than done, to be sure, when you realize the intensity of the self-esteem issues involved. I've yet to see the tendency to be self-critical sidestepped all at once, but I have seen it circumvented in a relatively brief period of time. Our difficulties aren't solved by circumventing them. Next, we have to deal with the pent-up frustration and anger directed toward a system that has had us inappropriately blaming ourselves for all the conflicts we've had with it. And what's more, we're now facing the conflicts, but without an apparent *means* for changing our relationships to the system. We must anticipate these feelings and be prepared to deal with them.

Another way of circumventing our lack of self-esteem is by agreeing in advance that we will temporarily drop whatever we are doing the first time a self-critical tendency is manifest in someone's characterization of a discrepancy. At this point, everyone needs to pitch in with reports of times when his self-critical nature got the best of him. We need to recall times that we were censored and accepted the blame, when actually both we and the organization were at fault. Such reports help us become less defensive about being defensive.

A Format for Explicating Discrepancies

We need structure for moving from feelings of incoherence to articulated discrepancies. We have to ask ourselves and others:

1. In what ways could this feeling of incoherence be a clue that the organization expects something from us that doesn't seem natural or consistent with our self-interests?
2. In what ways could this feeling of incoherence be a clue that something that seems natural enough to us is considered inappropriate or inadequate by the system?

Thus, in identifying discrepancies, the group's discussion begins with spontaneous reports of incoherent feelings. Members question one another, share accounts of personal experiences, and interact in any way that seems relevant to these two questions.

In addition to explicating discrepancies, this type of discussion has general educational value. Through the reports of others and their interaction with us, we will see instances where we've misidentified expectations or procedures and where we've missed seeing that our behavior was at odds with the organization system.

Consciousness-raising develops momentum as members take turns transforming feelings of incoherence into realized discrepancies. The object is not to identify an exhaustive list of discrepancies but to talk about those feelings of incoherence that are most strongly felt by individual members. One person's report may stimulate an entire meeting's discussion, with the result that a number, if not all, of those present will identify the discrepancy as his own. It's crucial to remember that the insights generated by group discussion are the meeting's product. However, it is also important to keep track of the discrepancies that sparked these insights, for they will provide the inputs for the next stage of consciousness-raising.

Reflection

As a list of discrepancies is evolved, support group members are likely to find themselves feeling better and better and more able to take constructive action to improve their relationships with the organization. At this point, each person will probably start making some changes in his own everyday activities. However, I advise continuing through at least the next stage of the consciousness-raising model before attempting any major improvements. Knowing the discrepancies in one's relationship to the organization system is not the same as knowing the system involved, and if one proceeds too hastily, one is likely to violate something, either in the organization or in oneself, that in turn ignites a repressive reaction.

CHAPTER 13

Stage 2:
Understanding
Ourselves and
the Organization

Discrepancies not only identify where we and the system are in conflict; they also help us to see aspects of ourselves and the organization that we had not previously recognized. They thus provide the starting point for our attaining an enhanced sense of personal identity and for discerning which organization goals and ideals are in our self-interests. They also provide the starting point for our discovering what the organization is and how it actually operates, what it wants from us, and how it acts to get it.

Our daily work experiences would reveal hidden perspectives of ourselves and the organization if we knew how to extract the tacit lessons that they contain. But most of us, most of the time, need additional skills and support to learn these lessons. In contrast to more established methods, such as various techniques of systems analysis and psychotherapy, the second stage of consciousness-raising provides us with a means for doing this with only a minimal reliance on experts.

This stage of consciousness-raising begins with discrepancies because they represent cracks in our socialization. Theoretically, any discrepancy we experience is an equally good starting place, because the same fundamental processes that characterize how we and the organization operate are present no matter where we start. Using our actual experience makes the quest interesting and practical. And our challenge is not just to learn from a specific experience, it is to learn *how to learn* from our experience. However, using discrepancies to begin a new stage of consciousness-raising and reflection goes against our natural inclinations to reduce conflict and solve problems. But just as new skills and support helped us resist inclinations to avoid feelings of incoherence, so new skills and support can help us counteract our inclinations to solve problems.

Skills

These skills are called skills for divergent problem-solving, in contrast to skills for convergent problem-solving. We are all quite familiar with and adept at convergent problem-solving. This is simply the process of accepting a particular problem more or less as presented and directing our thoughts and actions toward affecting a solution that makes sense in terms of that problem. The word convergent characterizes the problem-solving decisions we make as we converge toward a solution— not the range of solutions we consider. We can be convergent problem solvers even though we consider thousands of options at each decision-making step of a problem-solving process.

In convergent problem-solving, each decision takes us closer to the solution. Most managers and technical specialists are valued by their organizations for their skills in convergent problem solving. Organization life, particularly in the private sector, is action oriented. It demands quick thinking and an aggressive attitude toward solving problems. Delay, for whatever reason, is likely to result either in complaints, negative evaluations, or even in someone else stealing the problem right out from under us.

Divergent problem solving, on the other hand, requires different thought processes, which all of us use, although few of us use them skillfully. When we search for the meaning of an event rather than reacting concretely to the event itself, when we treat a problem-statement as if it were a symptom rather than a basic ill, when we inquire into the meaning of our differences with someone else, we use these thought processes. In essence, these are inductive skills that enable us to deepen the level at which problems are conceptualized. Let me illustrate with an example.

Example

Last year I attended a faculty meeting called by my dean to consider a petition signed by about half of the students in our new and experimental Professional Masters Program in Management. In advance of the meeting, the faculty was sent copies of the petition together with a covering letter from the dean explaining the problem as he saw it. The students were angry about the uneven quality of in-class teaching and the lack of out-of-class faculty availability. The dean stated that he had met with a representative group of petition signers and determined that they were conscientiously motivated and seriously concerned about the quality of the education they were receiving. Moreover, he stated, their complaints seemed well-founded. He urged all faculty members to attend the meeting, which, the letter explained, would be "an open discussion of what the faculty could do to upgrade the quality of their teaching activities."

Up to this point, the dean's actions typified the positive thinking and convergent problem-solving style used in most organizations. On the face of things, the issue seemed cut and dried. The faculty would simply come together and agree upon some approach for upgrading the quality of our teaching.

I was working on my model at this time, and all problem-statements were looking different to me. While I frequently experienced uneasiness about the agenda for faculty discussions, this time I was able to identify the reason. The students were reacting to discrepancies in our relationship to the academic system. Facing these discrepancies could lead to fundamental change, but the way we were formulating the problem made this unlikely. Our formulation would lead us to make adaptational changes that would merely cover over cracks in the present system. We were about to attack a symptom and miss the basic ill.

When this type of problem-solving approach is recognized in industry, it's called fire-fighting, and results in solutions that rid people of a problem only to have the underlying issues come back to haunt them in another form.

One other aspect of our dean's formulation of the problem caught my attention. In his eagerness to be responsive to student demands and upgrade the quality of our school's effectiveness, he had unintentionally left himself out of the problem. Serendipitiously for him, he had seized upon an old managerial strategy whereby the problem is formulated in such a way that the manager is put in a moral position—in this case, of being for quality education and for the students—without being a part of the problem.

I decided to call the dean, whom I like and respect, and tell him that I didn't think the meeting would work the way the problem had been formulated. Was I missing something? He replied that he thought some of the faculty were clearly guilty of classroom negligence and hoped that an open discussion would give them a chance to put themselves back on the right track. I told him that I thought the faculty would make better progress if the topic could be switched from solving the problem as he stated it to searching for the meaning of the petition. To make sure he got the point, I called attention to how his definition left him out of the problem. I suggested that we begin our discussion with a new divergent question: "What should we be learning about ourselves and our teaching system from the *fact* that this petition exists and that students feel in conflict with faculty?" At the end of our conversation, the dean seemed to understand my perspective and expressed appreciation for the call.

At our faculty meeting, the dean began the discussion by formulating the issue along the lines I had suggested. However, the difficulty in maintaining a divergent focus immediately became apparent. Despite the dean's best efforts, as well as my own attempts to help from the audience, the discussion took an irreversible convergent focus. We were back to the original problem; looking for ways to upgrade our teaching.

As the discussion developed, most of our faculty's comments communicated blame. Accepting that the problem was poor teaching, many suggested greater controls and punishments. Others expressed guilt, and a few tried to depersonalize the issue by blaming the curriculum design committee. Changes were proposed that promised to make the faculty game more subtle: we would appear to say yes to all requests for extra work and then handle our overload by giving perfunctory performances in activities of low personal priority. This is a common response of overworked people when confronted by additional job demands and no legitimate means for giving something else up.

We all knew who the players were. As it turned out, the unnamed guilty were the people suggesting impersonal solutions that would make their teaching deficiencies more difficult to spot. The unnamed not-guilty were the people proposing solutions that would increase their own work load. Of course, neither response would be good for the overall system. Uncommitted faculty have reasons for their indifference, and until these reasons are faced they are not going to change. Committed faculty run the risk of overburdening themselves and, in the long run, becoming casualties of the system. However, where else could we go with our self-imposed problem-statement and the convergent problem-solving tack we were taking?

A divergent problem-solving focus would have taken us in other directions. We might have raised such questions as:

- What can we make out of the fact that students take their complaints to administrators rather than the faculty who are the targets of their criticisms?
- What are the consequences of the dean acting as a third party in the student-defined conflict between themselves and the faculty?
- What does this petition tell us about the *real* priority that teaching has in the academic system?
- What conditions are required for all faculty, even the okay ones, to do better teaching?
- Are there ways that this petition can be viewed as a positive sign of our teaching program, i.e., that it signifies students are talking to one another and are involved?
- What forces within the system contribute to poor teaching?
- How can supports, rather than better personal defenses, be built for faculty who would like to do better, but don't know how?
- What does this petition tell us about how we're evaluating our experimental program?
- What prevents the faculty from talking publicly about their teaching at times other than crisis?
- In what ways do students contribute to their own problems?

These questions are illustrative of the numerous opportunities that the small discrepancies of daily living give us to learn about ourselves and the organization system. It's mind-boggling to realize how many discrepancies are lost in the process of getting work done. Such opportunities for learning are destroyed by converging too quickly. On the other hand, a faculty study group could, in this case, easily spend many months divergently analyzing the meaning of the students' petition without doing anything either to improve the quality of teaching or to deal with the immediate problem posed by a disgruntled group of students.

The dilemma, therefore, is in striking a balance between getting something done fast and in having a longer period of time for divergent analysis before taking action. How do we determine when the situation demands that we stop our divergent analysis, reformulate the problem based on our best thinking to that time, and get on with the implementation? And how do we determine that we've improved our problem formulation to the point where it allows us to grapple with some fundamental aspect of the people and systems involved?

Support

We need support to resist our impulse to take immediate corrective action when we move from a feeling of incoherence to the formulation of a discrepancy in our relationship with a system. For instance, in the preceding example, our dean's first impulse when he noted the discrepancy between our school's ideal of teaching excellence and the experiences that students were having was to correct things by getting faculty to upgrade their teaching. Delaying action for further study, once a legitimate problem has been recognized, entails living with new internal anxieties: "Something is off, and I could be doing something about it." It also means living with new external pressures: "Other people know I'm aware that something is off, and they'll interpret my inaction as a lack of concern about a problem that matters to them." Thus, not acting upon discrepancies means living with new anxieties and tensions. This is a difficult task for a single individual, it is not nearly so difficult with the help of a support group.

In cases of extreme pressure, support group members can help us figure out a holding action for coping with a troublesome situation. The problem with holding actions, though, is that frequently we get taken in by them. Having dealt with the immediate pressures, we forget to go back and learn from the original discrepancy. By explicit agreement, support group members can help us back to tension areas that have been set aside, as well as support our inaction on issues that can wait.

Reflection

This stage of the consciousness-raising model helps us learn about aspects of ourselves and the organization system that are obscured by conventional ways of interacting with the system. Acquiring this knowledge requires support and a structure that fosters divergent reasoning. We'll need a good deal of openness and emotional discipline, because by dealing with discrepancies much of what is learned goes counter to current images of ourselves and the system. Absorbing the tensions produced by this dissonance requires structure: one that helps us attain sufficient abstraction to foster objectivity, but keeps us focused on issues of practical relevance.

CHAPTER 14

Group Support for Stage 2

There's nothing complex about the process of divergent reasoning. Any question that gets people to probe deeply into the conditions that underlie a dis crepancy, or to inquire into the assumptions that underlie a problem situation, provides a structure that helps us reason inductively. A starting question might be, "What does the mere existence of this particular discrepancy tell us about ourselves, about the system?" or "If this discrepancy is a symptom of something more basic, what human qualities and organization attributes could have produced it.

Divergent reasoning requires inductive skills that we all possess, but when we're anxious and up against a problem, we need support to use them. When our boss is picking on us, these skills allow us to consider what's wrong with the organization chart and with our boss's relationship to his boss. However, more often than not, such situations blind us with anger. How can we be analytic when we're being so unjustly treated? At these times, we've got to protect ourselves and fight back however we can, perhaps even unfairly.

Our support group needs to develop a structure that helps us remain divergent. The specific structure need not be very elaborate, as long as each member agrees to it. The structure should carry us beyond the aggressiveness that gets aroused when we're viewing some system characteristic that has been hemming us in and the defensiveness we exhibit when being exposed to some aspect of ourselves that is less than our ideal. Members of our group will need to find other ways to support one another than through expressions of empathy. We'll also need to give support through honest confrontation and challenge.

Group Process

Prior to starting this second stage of consciousness-raising, I suggest that two people be assigned the task of recording what is learned, one person writing down what is learned about support group members, the other writing down what is learned about organization systems. They record simple sentences like "I think the organization has a fairly accurate picture of what's ahead for my career," and "The system has no means of maintaining a memory for personnel plans that extend beyond a two-year period." It is preferable for these recorders to write their statements on large pieces of newsprint so that misinterpretations can be spotted immediately and modified. Once the discussion gets rolling, we will find many differences about how a statement should be phrased. When these differences persist, the group's momentum can be maintained by noting alongside a particular statement the initials of those who don't think it applies to them.

It's best to begin consciousness-raising with a discrepancy that a number of group members have identified as important to them. Usually, such a discrepancy is current; so people will be looking for some resolution. For example, a group of people who have just been promoted might begin with "Here we've just been promoted and we're feeling depressed!"

Because a coordinator is necessary to maintain a divergent discussion, I recommend keeping his duties similar to those suggested in the preceding stage and rotating the job each meeting. In addition, the coordinator should try to help group members who are being cut off, make sure summary statements get recorded, bring out minority perspectives, give members who fail to see the relevance of some insight a chance to say why, and generally keep everyone aware of the topic under discussion.

Discrepancies are like the early insights produced in psychoanalysis, the same insights that prompt the analyst to caution his patient about precipitous actions. The analyst knows that early expressions of new consciousness are likely to be displacements, whereby wives or husbands take the rap for conflicts more accurately attributed to parents. Analogously, others in our support group can often see ahead and sense that additional probing will turn up a more fundamental definition of our problem. For instance, if we raise the convergent complaint that "The ideals that prompted me to work in government are inevitably compromised by red tape," others can challenge us to think more expansively. They will confront us with a divergent focus that takes us beyond our myopic solutions. They can remind us of instances when someone's ideals were strong enough to break through the red tape. They can educate us about parts of the system that we have overlooked. And they can point out how our overinflated self-image makes us uncompromising. We need not abstain from convergent processes for an indefinite period of time, just until divergent analysis has been attempted.

Our next challenge occurs when we return to our jobs after a group meeting and see in operation the very problems we've been talking about, even though we do not yet understand them fully. While the most sensible tactic is a holding action, we'll be tempted to straighten matters out on the spot. Support group members can help with these situations by discussing the practical consequences of our insights. For example, they can point out that twenty years of interagency bickering is not resolved in a day.

The extent to which a discrepancy is probed and the amount of time we spend discussing it cannot be specified in advance. Moreover, switching the topic is not necessarily the appropriate response to boredom or lethargy, frequent signs of avoidance. What we are avoiding can usually be identified if someone asks the group a divergent question, such as, "If we weren't so lethargic, what might we be talking about?" Likewise, how far a group can push a resistant or blocked member is also a matter of judgment and experience with that person. Personal resistances to consciousness are important for a support group to confront. It's a well-documented fact that our most important insights are preceded by periods of argumentation and defensiveness, as if we have to exhaust every trick in our personality before owning up to the realization.

As a matter of principle, I'm for the architectural rights of each person to construct his own personal realities and not be beaten into submission by others who see things differently. Also as a matter of principle, I'm for each support group member to take on the subcontractor's obligation to understand someone's blueprints sufficiently well to notice when he's overlooked something important. It's not enough for us to walk away feeling we've said our piece when we know the other person hasn't actually comprehended it. In practice, these two perspectives will cause conflict. We will see issues that we think apply to someone else, but he may resist. How we debate these differences will crucially effect the tone of our support group.

At moments of conflict, I fall back on the belief that different realities are the products of different experiences. When we are the target of someone else's reality, it feels much better if that person tells us about his own experience and refrains from making criticisms of us. We don't want to hear that we are aggressive and cutting; we prefer to hear that when he is listening to us he feels hurt and reticent to talk. It is possible that we are acting differently than we think. But until we decide which is more accurate, the other person can make things easier for us by admitting that it is his perception he is relating rather than some quality of ours. In our minds, we don't yet know if he's super-sensitive or if we're coming on too strong. It is when we feel others are trying to categorize us on the basis of a single experience, or are making inferences about our pictures of reality, based on how *they* feel in a similar situation, that we get uptight about feedback.

We're obviously going to have some disagreements about how we see ourselves and the organization. Disagreements about how we see the organization will be the easiest ones to resolve. Wherever possible, we can formulate small experiments and go out into the organization to collect data relevant to resolving our differences. For instance, someone says, "You're kidding yourself. No one who has ever been a shipping manager for more than five years has ever received another promotion." Resolving this may require no more than asking the guys in your car pool what they think, or it can be as elaborate as tracking down and interviewing people who have been shipping managers.

Informal experiments are also useful in resolving differences about how we see ourselves in the organization. But in such experiments, it's much more difficult to agree on what constitutes a fair test and interpretation of the data. In either case, it's important to remember that we're observing a moving target that changes over time and under different conditions.

Reflection

This second stage of consciousness-raising is aimed at producing more awareness about our own nature and ideals and about the nature of the system and how it actually works. Having a better perspective on reality allows us to exercise greater control over our organization life and relate more appropriately to the present system. But we may still be hard pressed to make any fundamental changes in our relationship to it.

We don't yet know the assumptions that lead others in the system to control certain rights that we think belong to us, and we're not yet sure why we're motivated to want what we do. If we tried to change things too much, we'd probably meet with extraordinary resistance. Thus, knowing the systems involved is not all there is to having more freedom, even though it gives us much more control. Further control of our organization life depends on the extent to which we comprehend the reasons why we and the system operate the way we do. We need to know the assumptions that explain our current patterns of interacting with the system, and we have to discover real alternatives to present practices.

CHAPTER 15

Stage 3: Understanding Our Relationship with the Organization

It's one thing to have insights that allow us to comprehend our nature and the organization system, but it takes another level of probing to weave what we've learned into a perspective that allows us to initiate a change in our relationship with the system. Ultimately, gaining control depends on discovering the assumptions that underlie our participation in the system. Let me illustrate what I'm talking about with an example about a manager named George. At one time or another, George had all the insights needed to understand what he wanted and what the organization system was demanding of him, but he did not understand his relationship with the organization well enough to exert much influence over his life.

Example

George retired recently at the age of fifty-seven, although most of his associates contended that he informally retired years ago. George worked thirty-five years for his company, first as a technical specialist and later as a manager in his specialty. George never rose above the middle-managerial level, but a generous retirement program and wise investments on his part made him worth half a million dollars at the time of his retirement.

I met George about three years before he retired. He had just been relieved of his managership and transferred to a planning and budgeting function. George took over his new job from a female administrative assistant earning one-third his salary. Although the job was expanded somewhat when George took over, and there was a lot of hoopla about how, "At last our division is going to get serious about a crucial but overlooked aspect of its operations," everyone knew, including George (I asked him), that this was the last step in shoving him aside to make room for a "more aggressive and technically competent man."

George was about as thoroughly socialized an organization manager as you'd ever want to see in a white shirt and bow tie. He had a positive attitude, reacted obediently to organizational directives, performed dull tasks without complaining, and never hesitated to work late or on weekends when facing a deadline. When he was younger, George was usually able to see things management's way, while acknowledging that, taken at face value, some things didn't quite make sense. As he grew older, he became "good ol' George," who had a smile and pleasantry for everyone he encountered.

Retiring before you're sixty-two is unusual in George's company, no matter how much money you've salted away. In talking with George, I realized that this wasn't his first choice either, but he was feeling useless because he knew he'd never again play an essential role in the organization. Then one day, George's boss asked him how he was fixed financially and if he might consider an early retirement. George said, "I'll think about it," and after a couple of months he announced, "I want to do it this year." The boss said, "I'll get back to you." But when George waited several weeks without hearing anything, he got fighting mad and threatened to quit. His boss told me, "George took me by surprise. That was the first time I'd ever seen him lose his cool, and we had to quickly give him the facts of life."

There is an Internal Revenue Service rule that can severely penalize an employee who retires or quits voluntarily before the age of sixty. Because George could have lost much of what he accumulated in the company's retirement plan, the company's delay was caused by their need to make sure that he could retire with the proper tax treatment.

If he didn't, this would create unnecessary anxiety for others in the organization. For George to get his full pension, it was essential that the company formally retire him on the grounds that he was no longer technically competent to hold his job. But this wasn't good for George or the organization. It would embarrass George and mar the company's image of job security. Therefore, while George was officially fired, everyone inside the company was allowed to think he quit. However, to an outsider, the discrepancy was apparent. When I asked George's boss how people could be cheerful at George's retirement party, he replied, "At the time of the party, only I and a small part of George's mind realized the truth."

In reflecting on George's situation, the issue of his supposed incompetence stuck in my mind. How does a person like George become progressively devalued to the point where he is first shoved aside and then squeezed out all together? According to George, it was a combination of the company exploiting his talents by keeping him on dull jobs that were bread-and-butter money producers and of his personal cowardice to quit the company after the handwriting was on the wall. George added, ". . . you've also got to consider that I was raised in a regime where Papa knew best. He's the boss and he knows. Once in a while, I'd think about being more aggressive along the lines of demanding a transfer or some additional training, but I always felt that wouldn't be the politic thing to do."

I asked a high-level manager who knew George for his ideas about how such a relationship develops between a man and an organization. This particular manager is among my favorites, and I enjoy his crisp if somewhat bald way of saying things. He said, "Guys like George get identified very early. Each man is hired because the company thinks he has the potential to go right up the line. Within a year or two, you know all about the guy. If anybody says he doesn't, he's lying. It's at this point that the first mistake is made. Rather than fire him, it's rationalized, 'This man needs another assignment. He needs experience with another manager.' Between the second and fifth years, more doubts are expressed and suppressed. It's said like this, 'We owe it to the company to give him another chance.' At the end of the fifth year, the company has painted itself into a corner. The man gets transferred to a noncritical area. Every company has its sink traps where the insolubles are collected before they're swept down the drain. In our company, the sink traps are planning and budgeting, management development, packing and shipping, and other rinky-dink jobs. Then you say, 'This guy isn't going to make it, but he is only two years from having his retirement benefits vested.' By the time he's entitled to his retirement fund, the guy is in his midthirties, and it's your last chance to move him out. Then it's sheer procrastination that keeps him around. It's then that the company does its paternalistic thing. They condemn him to a lifetime of mediocrity in the guise of doing the fair thing for him. But it's too late. These guys wind up sitting around working crossword puzzles and talking about their farms in the country."

I asked this manager if he had any ideas for improving things. "The important thing," he answered, "is to identify these guys as soon as possible, at least during the third to fifth years, and get them back on the road. The problem is the missionary syndrome of those who sit around trying to rehabilitate a guy who has failed in another area. If you succeed, then you score in every possible category. The whole board lights up. If you fail, you can always blame it on someone else who should have fired him long before the guy got to you. We create the image that once you're processed by personnel you're set for life, but eventually we have to mop up the consequences."

Returning to George, one might reason that with more on the ball or more support he would have fared better. He might have faced up to his own feelings of growing stale and resisted organization requests to stay on a job he had manned for years. The fact of the matter is that he did try to do this for a while. George told me that "as early as 1955 I was feeling unhappy about the slowness with which my career was unfolding. I was at a low point in my feelings about the job and the company. I went to my boss and told him that I thought a change would be good for me. He seemed interested enough at the time, but didn't do anything. After a while, I stopped resenting him. I remember feeling, 'Where could I go and be as good, unless I went to work for a competitor?' But then I reasoned that that wouldn't be right. I even went to one of those head-hunting organizations, but the alternatives didn't look so good. I didn't want to be considered by a competitor; I don't know quite why, but it just didn't seem ethical. So fifteen years later, I was still on the same job."

Even if George in fact lacked the aggressiveness and technical know-how to succeed in another managerial job or elsewhere in his company, he would have been much better off if he had faced the facts and figured out what, if anything, he might do to improve things. With this understanding, he could even have turned around and made the same decisions that were made de facto for him by the company. He might then have come to an early retirement feeling good about his organization career instead of leaving with a feeling of impotence.

However, George was at a power disadvantage, and out of control of his organization career. While he had a fair degree of self-understanding and had been around long enough to know how the organization really worked, he lacked the skills for uncovering the assumptions on which his relationship with the company were based.

I think that with a better understanding of his relationship to the organization, George could have had a much better fate. By the way, George's retirement is anything but the Sun City story you might expect if you viewed him from the organization's perspective. It is one of venture and risk. A few years ago, he bought a farm that is being worked by a tenant farmer. George is in the process of developing more of his acreage, and has begun a profitable real estate business on the side. Since leaving the company, he has added considerably to his expertise in both these ventures. To me, his post-company accomplishments conflict dramatically with his manager's contention that he was too passive and technically obsolete to make any further contributions to the company. You might reason, "Well with a small fortune socked away, what kind of risk is George taking now?" True enough, but with the same financial security, he failed to take risks on the company's time. And even if he were obsolete to his company, no doubt there was a point when explicitly confronting the organization's view of him could have made a difference in George's career.

Our Interaction with the Organization

While I've heard many arguments about how productivity would go to hell if we were more in control of our organization lives, I've yet to hear someone argue that he personally would not like more control. Recently, a high-level manager told me, "When I hear that top management is making plans for someone, I feel confident that they will make decisions that are constructive, effective, and good for the man. But when I hear that the someone they're planning for is me, then I get worried!" Continuing, the manager expressed concern that, "Top management can't possibly have a complete or accurate picture of what I want, particularly when you stop to consider that their thinking is optimized around organization priorities, as if nothing else in my life mattered."

Increased understanding of our relationship with the organization means greater clarity about where it leaves off and where we begin. This involves searching out the assumptions that underlie our interactions with the organization. First, we must explicate these assumptions, and next, we must figure out where they came from or how we acquired them. Eventually, we'll want to reconsider the ways we participate in the organization, but we'll have a hard time formulating alternatives, let alone putting them into action, until we understand which assumptions conflict with our nature and our ideals. Basically, we'll have to search for assumptions in three areas.

The first area encompasses the goals we hold and how we go about achieving them. This includes the goals that determine our present behavior as well as our long-term career objectives. Most people seem fairly articulate about their short-term goals and how they're accomplishing them, but few seem to know much about the origins of these goals and their personal preferences for how to proceed.

The second area encompasses the assumptions we make about our own organization system. This includes its purpose, values, and role, and, particularly, its way of viewing us. People can usually be pushed into stating the assumptions they make about the organization, but when questioned about whether or not their assumptions are valid, they say, "It doesn't make any difference whether or not they're valid, they are practical; so what's the use of questioning further?!" In my experience, there is a lot to be gained by questioning further.

The third area encompasses the ways we and the organization influence one another. This means identifying the areas of communication we can trust and rely on as being accurate. It also means facing up to the evasiveness, the manipulations, the half-truths, the impressions, the use of power, and the informal coalitions that characterize our interactions with the system. This is an area in which most people have more awareness and more realistic perspectives about someone else than they have about themselves. Some people considerably overestimate the influence they exercise in their organization life, and others consistently underestimate it.

AREA 1: Assumptions Underlying Goals and
Ways We Accomplish Them

Raising consciousness about the assumptions underlying our goals and the way we go about accomplishing them can be achieved in many settings. Not so long ago, to take one instance, three hundred and fifty first-year students in my school's Professional Master's Program in Management were assigned a paper to be handed in at the beginning of the *first* day of class. These papers would be graded and could comprise anywhere from one-fifth to one-third of a student's grade in the course. To the best of my knowledge, not one of these many students complained about having part of his grade based on a paper written before teaching began. The goal of many students who came to class was limited to learning what they needed to know to be successful in the business world and get certified by the university. Their concept of success meant getting an *A* in the classroom. If the system said "Write a paper," they would do so, and they would try to believe that this constituted learning. This would not have been possible if they had identified the assumptions that underlay their relationship to the school. At this point in their careers, the school was the organization system, and understanding their relationship to it meant being conscious of the assumptions contained in their educational goals and in the ways they learned.

Another example, this one in a different setting, concerns a manager who was told fifteen years ago by his boss that his flamboyant style irritated too many people, and he shouldn't plan on going any further up the company ladder. This was despite the fact that he possessed one of the best "chemical minds" in the company. Like George, the man who retired, this manager assessed his prospects outside his company and decided that his chance of improving on what he already had wasn't worth the risk of quitting. So in order to save face for himself, he became even more flamboyant and provocative when interacting with his boss, and he continued this style with subsequent bosses. This manager did not sufficiently understand his relationship with his company to know why he needed to provoke all his bosses. He was not at all provocative with subordinates, with whom he developed a reputation as a patient and outstanding developer of people. However, subordinates did resent him for his inability to get promoted and make room for their advancement.

AREA 2: Assumptions We Make
about the Organization

The students in our Professional Master's Program and the flamboyant manager would have benefited from consciousness-raising about the assumptions they were making about the organization. The students were acting as if a passive-compliant stance in the classroom would fulfill the faculty's need to teach as well as their need to relate course material to their individual interests. They seemed to assume either that they did not need to get involved in the planning of classwork or that the faculty didn't want their involvement and would penalize them for meddling. In my discussion section, the lid came off when I began the first class by chastising those twenty-two out of twenty-six who had prepared the written assignment, and I went on to express my discomfort with other assumptions that typically link students and faculty. The students argued with one another, some criticized me, and many got quite emotional. They were experiencing signs of what I call structure shock, the wave of anxiety that sweeps over a person when he realizes that he is in a situation that makes little sense and has no intrinsic order until he asserts his own interests into the situation. I was questioning conventional classroom roles and wouldn't yield to those who felt I was destructively ungluing things. One by one, the students began declaring their own goals and in the process identified with other students who had overlapping interests. The class evolved its own format, with students bringing their own interests and priorities to assignments. Let's take, for example, a written assignment in the area of *complex systems.* Why should a student interested in real estate have to write his paper on the energy crisis like everyone else? Thus in my class students felt the latitude to interact with their assignments and make them relevant to their own personal goals and priorities. Incidentally, I received informal censure from some of my colleagues who felt I was deserting the team and disapproval from students in other sections who felt my students might have a competitive advantage in grading.

In the other situation, the flamboyant manager had apparently transferred his reaction from his original boss to all successive bosses and to most authority relationships he had in the organization. His story prompted me to do some searching. I discovered that the man who told him he'd never be promoted was generally dismissed as a member of the old school, and had retired two years after delivering the fatal message. I also learned that while the flamboyant manager appeared somewhat unruly at that time, this was not a companywide perception; thus, his overreaction to his admonishment produced a self-fulfilling effect. At the time I got involved, this man was a young fifty, and it seemed there was still time for things to change, if only he could connect with some of the assumptions he was making about the organization, particularly its view of him, and test them out explicitly.

AREA 3: Assumptions Underlying How We and the Organization Influence One Another

Finally, the students as well as the manager could benefit from identifying the ways they and the organization influenced each other. As long as the students in our Master's Program assumed that they were single individuals trying to get through the educational system in the best way they could, they were reduced to personally dealing with every situation presented to them. When the rule didn't fit them, their only recourse was to find a sympathetic teacher or administrator and persuade him to give them special consideration. Their individual relationships with the organization caused them to think in terms of their own needs rather than in terms of policies and procedures that affect a class of people. Only when students become aware of the elitist and competitive assumptions underlying their attempts to circumvent irrelevant requirements or debate unfair grades will they be able to search for alternative ways of making the system more relevant to their interests. Some students did figure this out eventually, and they began working cooperatively for curriculum reforms. They organized petitions that were signed by some members of the faculty and administration, and invented a procedure for periodically meeting with instructors to brief them on their interests.

Normally, I don't look upon the consultant's role as one of making good things happen for people. Rather I try to help people take charge of their own lives and make good things happen for themselves. However, with the flamboyant manager, I knew no other way of helping but to personally confront him with the possibility that some of his assumptions had gone too long without being tested. I had known this man for a couple of years, and I think that at the time of my confrontation he counted me as a member of his informal support system. I suggested that if he were still interested he might ask his current boss whether or not he was still judged unpromotable and under what conditions he might be considered for promotion. After weeks of deliberation, he decided to take up my challenge. However, his current boss apparently had also become exasperated with him and responded with double-talk just to get him out of his hair. I next urged him to take this issue to his boss's boss, a company vice-president. Going along with my suggestion constituted a company no-no on two counts. First, one does not make an end-run around one's boss, and second, vice-presidents are not to be *bothered* with personal matters. But he finally made it to the vice-president, and within two weeks was transferred to another department. The company hopes that he will have better relationships there and eventually be considered for promotion.

Reflection

Each of the stories related in this chapter is about the same basic problem. George, the students in our Master's Program, and the flamboyant manager were each suffering from inadequate understanding of the relationships they had formed with the organization system. Explicating the assumptions underlying their relationship with the system helped the students and the flamboyant manager exert more control over their organization life. In George's case, it was too late.

My intervention in these events can be criticized as being specific to unique problems. The students were helped to take more control over their two years of learning at the university, but the question remains whether or not they will be able to invent the supports to exert similar kinds of control after they leave school. The flamboyant manager got a second chance by taking one more provocative action. Did this merely reinforce the type of action that will again be his undoing, setting him up for what eventually will be an even bigger disappointment? Anything positive that came out of my interacting with these people was due to their comprehension of previously unexplicated assumptions that underlay their relationships with the organization.

Successes such as these are likely to prove momentary against the context of a lifetime, unless the underlying principles are grasped and converted to perspectives that people can use to initiate improvements for themselves. I believe that consultants and teachers should limit their exposure to consciousness-raising to demonstration projects, and the skills and supports that help us do this should be practiced in our own support group.

CHAPTER 16

Group Support for Stage 3

We are now ready to rethink our relationship with the organization and put it on a more realistic plane. There are four steps to doing this. First, we identify the assumptions that characterize our interactions with the organization system. Second, we contrast these assumptions against current experiences and newly acquired insights to see if they fit. If they do, we can validate our existing picture of reality. Third, we discard assumptions that no longer fit and bring our pictures of reality up to date by substituting assumptions that are more consistent with our present experience and understanding.

The fourth step is of a slightly different order. It involves recalling how we acquired those assumptions that didn't fit. We do this in an effort to learn more about situations that render us susceptible to having realities imposed on us. For instance, we may recall how we learned never to write reports in the first person, but instead to use colorless, impersonal jargon. Thinking about how we learned this will produce some of the most revealing insights into our organization life, for it will help us see exactly how the organization goes about influencing us. We will recall diverse experiences ranging from an orientation period we spent reading the files to the time when our first boss bawled us out for slipping a harmless pun into a department report. While it's unrealistic to think that we'll be able to use what we learn to devise a foolproof defense against such influences, we can at least increase our chances of knowing what's happening to us, and so recognize more easily when it's time to put up a fight.

While some relatively simple techniques are the only new skills needed for this third stage of consciousness-raising, the corresponding group supports are fairly complex. More so than in any of the previous stages we have discussed, group members will need to probe the implicit meanings of what is said, challenge one another, and be strict about observing procedures. Confronting how we've been socialized by the system can produce feelings of anger and frustration that can side-track a group. To gain objectivity, the group will need to look outside itself, cross-checking its viewpoints with others and with events occurring in the organization. This will require discipline and follow-up.

The Group Process

By the time our group reaches this stage of consciousness-raising, it's a good idea not to add new members if we can possibly avoid it. If we do, the benefits they receive are likely to be overshadowed by the oppressiveness of their relating to realities that they had no part in building. If for some reason our group feels compelled to include some-one new, I'd recommend that he limit his participation to staying on the sidelines and watching us work. Let him observe what insights have meaning to us, making his own decision about whether or not they apply to him.

It's a good idea to begin each meeting by reviewing what we hope to accomplish and what we need to do to accomplish it. The meeting's process will be further enhanced if we know in advance that there will be time at the end of the meeting to consider modifications for the next session. After such an orientation, we are set to begin.

Actual consciousness-raising begins with group members taking turns describing the assumptions they make. Members listen to one another and assess the extent to which they identify with what's being said. Any discussion that takes place should be directed toward helping group members clarify and sharpen what they are saying. We have already mentioned the three areas that need to be explored. These are (1) our short- and long-term goals and how we accomplish them; (2) our image of the organization system; and (3) our ways of influencing the organization and the ways the organization influences us.

For example, we can help others explicate assumptions they make in the first area by asking them to state their goals for personal success and fulfillment, inquiring why these particular goals are meaningful to them, and questioning how they plan to go about achieving them. As they talk, we listen for the "as-if" and "if-then" messages that seem to be contained in what they say.

Thus, a consciousness-raising session on the topic of career goals, for example, prompted one person to say, "I think that one should do whatever he does as well as possible and have faith that it will be recognized as good. At the same time, I realize that justice doesn't always seem to be present." The speaker was talking *as if* he didn't need to influence the criteria used in judging him, that they would be sufficiently flexible to appreciate his efforts. But his assumptions about justice seemed fatalistic: *if* he was not treated fairly, *then* there was little he could do about it.

When the discussion switched to the topic of how to achieve career goals, someone else said, "The way to get along in this company is to look good in your boss's eyes and not worry too much about what you look like in your peers' eyes." There are a multitude of assumptions embedded in this statement, beginning with the implications it holds for the quality of work performance and the enjoyment of one's job, and extending to the type of self-alienation and convergent problem-solving processes that such assumptions stimulate.

After a number of assumptions have been generated, it's advisable to poll group members on the extent of their conscious identification with each one. I suggest that the discussion leader mark down next to each assumption the number of group members who strongly feel, "Yes, that's me!" the number who think, "That's me some of the time," the number who think, "That could be me, but I don't feel like it." Assumptions that evoke only minimal feelings are probably not quite on target and should be dropped from the present discussion. If the issues contained in them are important, they probably will come up later. Assumptions that evoke strong identification from only one or two individuals usually have unique histories and contain special learning opportunities for the individuals involved. I will shortly comment on how a group might deal with these. In testing whether or not the assumptions we're making fit with actual experience, we begin with those that have evoked strong feelings from a number of members. First, we identify the situations in which we've felt these assumptions in operation, and then we evaluate their effects. For each assumption whose effects seem positive, we have the chance to affirm and personally acknowledge it as characterizing our relationship with the organization. An assumption we judge as leading to undesirable consequences will trigger anger and motivate us to search for a substitute that better reflects our interests.

As we spend time identifying assumptions, affirming those that seem to fit and replacing those that don't, we will generate a list of invalid assumptions. During a separate meeting, these assumptions give us a special opportunity to learn about aspects of the organization that can influence us without our knowing it. We need to recall the conditions that existed when they were acquired.

Figuring out what was going on when an invalid assumption was acquired proceeds most easily when group members trade stories about where they first acted on a particular assumption. Sometimes we won't be able to track an assumption to its origin. In such cases, it may be sufficient to think of current instances in which it plays a prominent role in determining our activities. In either case, we'll want to recall the primary advocates of the assumption, what it does for the organization and the people involved, and the conditions when it seemed to be most applicable.

While we can expect gaps in any one person's account, the collection of stories will produce a relatively complete and accurate picture of the organizational dynamics involved. Our most accurate and objective pictures will come from discussing the genesis of a discarded assumption with which many group members expressed a strong identification.

Discussion Style To Circumvent Defensiveness

An assumption with which only one or two members strongly identified probably has a unique link to the personal history of those who identify with it. Regardless of where it comes from, the assumption is playing a critical role in determining someone's picture of reality, and its source will need to be identified if that person is to develop control over it. However, we are likely to encounter defensiveness and distrust when trying to assist others in figuring out their reasons for holding onto an idiosyncratic assumption.

There is a thin line between this person's feeling that we're trying to help him contact something real and his feeling that we are trying to categorize him inappropriately. To minimize such suspicions, our meeting format requires flexibility. The person struggling with the idiosyncratic assumption needs to feel our sensitivity to his unique reality. In such situations, it's important that the person involved figure out for himself the origin of the assumption. The group's role is to establish a supportive climate and to help design small experiments that the person making the assumption can carry out during his daily activities in the organization.

It's seldom possible to keep the atmosphere emotionally clean when we have our own ideas about the origin of an idiosyncratic assumption. However, we can keep extraneous conflict to a minimum by thinking and talking in terms of different perspectives on reality. We should describe the personal experiences that form the basis of our beliefs as well as inquire into the experiences that explain why the other person thinks differently. Moreover, even when there's group concensus about a blind spot in someone's self-perception, it's not wise for everyone to gang up on him. An openness to feedback is created when at least some group members play supportive roles; thus, both confrontation and support are needed—confrontation of the person's resistance to accurately hearing and examining what's being said to him, not confrontation aimed at getting him to agree with it, and support for the person's difficulties in actively considering what's being said to him, not insincere support for his point of view. For example, the supporter might turn to the person who is being confronted and say, "I don't see John making much progress in getting his point across to you. Do you have any ideas for changing the way you and he are talking so he at least feels like you've understood and considered what he's said?"

It's important that the person receiving feedback sees himself as at least co-directing the discussion. I sometimes say to him, "Suppose John is only three percent accurate in what he's saying about you, can you recall at least one instance that does apply to you?" After the recall of even a single instance, I'm ready to drop the issue, because once someone has seen a glimmer of an aspect of himself that is presently unacceptable to his self-image, he has the chance of seeing it in future situations. Time is an important factor when a person is determining the validity of what's been said to him or when he is deciding how far he wants to generalize its applicability. It's not uncommon for some insights to take hold after a dormant period of two or three years.

Let's now return to instances in which most group members feel a high degree of identification to a particular assumption. Usually, we are able to track down where and how such assumptions were acquired. The scene is now set for group members to consider taking action.

While I strongly believe that people should be left to come up with their own individual course of action, I also believe that group members can be helpful to one another. For example, after one of these consciousness-raising sessions, a group member went out to test the possibility that he may have been *in*correct in assuming that his organization put caution and precedent ahead of risk-taking and creativity. He had been assuming that the most crucial aspect of his job was to follow established procedures and not make mistakes. Group discussion persuaded him to recheck his assumption. Two weeks later, he told the group, "I went out and proposed something creative that I'm convinced would save the company thousands of dollars. But in the process, it meant shooting a sacred cow of twenty years' standing. My action incited a series of meetings from the top down to me. I was questioned until I finally rescinded my proposal and staggered away mumbling, 'I'll never do something like this again!' " Group members empathized with his experience and actively discussed whether or not other people were having different experiences. Pooling their knowledge, they counseled him not to become cynical or stop thinking creatively and suggested he transfer to another department, one which others in the group had experienced as more responsive to new ideas.

Reflection

This stage of consciousness-raising helps us straighten out those pictures of reality that bear on our personal relationship with the organization. However, this only gives us part of the picture. We also need to identify complementary assumptions that make up the pictures of reality held in other prominent parts of the organization. Unless we deal with those who see things differently, we run the risk of having them oppose the changes we want to make. Essentially, we're trying to put ourselves through a self-directed resocialization process in order that we might live our organization life with the minimal number of externally imposed adaptations. Our success depends on our anticipating where the pockets of resistance are likely to be and whether or not there's a way of getting around them without compromising what we want to express. Adding to our skills for doing this is the subject of the next chapter.

CHAPTER 17

Stage 4: Moving toward a More Natural Life in the Organization

Each time I hear about an obvious improvement in the personnel practices of an organization, I wonder how the people affected by the change were able to go so long without it. The issue is the same whether a change involves something as obvious and universal as equal work rights for minorities or something as subtle and specific as flexible working hours for a professional group. No doubt, some people realized the change was needed before it took place. But usually, most do not. Once the change is instituted, most of those who did not know it was needed realize its relevance to them and embrace its benefits. But by then they've missed their chance to exercise control. As I've emphasized throughout this book, an essential step in gaining control is our *own* envisioning of alternatives. When someone else takes the action that improves our lot, we may enjoy the immediate benefits, but we don't necessarily become more free.

Not all the alternatives we envision will be practical for the organization. However, the practicality of any specific alternative cannot be determined until it's been formulated. And organizations are inclined to fight us because they don't trust our alternatives to include organization concerns for productivity and viability in a changing environment. So, while we are denied the information we need to intelligently consider organization interests, our proposals are criticized as impractical and we are chastised for being uninformed. When we propose an alternative, we are expected to make a foolproof defense.

On the other hand, management will try to convince us that the system continually changes in response to our needs. They will point out numerous instances of job enrichment, whereby we're allowed to plan our workday, participate in decisions, switch jobs, communicate with fellow workers, expand the scope of our responsibilities, and, in general, experience a greater democratization of our work life. Yet most of these changes are carried out within the confines of an autocratic structure. Someone else decides which privileges and opportunities are allowed us; someone else determines whether or not we've adopted pictures of reality that will put these opportunities to the proper use.

There are already plenty of proposals for change around. Some of these begin with economic models, some with consumer concerns, some with human attributes, and some with managerial effectiveness. But most of us, most of the time, have tremendous difficulties recognizing which of these proposals meet our interests. Consequently, we often react passively, with low-keyed negativism that wears down those who have good ideas. We need the skills to discern fundamental from adaptational change, and the skills to penetrate the rhetoric that clouds such proposals. With these skills we could determine whether or not a particular proposal was based on assumptions that more closely parallel our interests than existing practices, and we could then endorse it energetically. Lacking these skills, we reject proposals that yield fundamental improvements and are taken in by proposals that increase our benefits and privileges, but not our rights.

This is exactly what happened to the auto workers who struck General Motors in 1970. Their primary purpose was to combat trends toward inhuman jobs, epitomized by installations of high-speed assembly lines like the one at Lordstown, Ohio, which was built to turn out one hundred Chevrolet Vegas per hour. Work on this line could be as robotlike as tightening three bolts per car, one hundred cars per hour. The strike neted workers a retroactive pay increase and enhanced retirement benefits, but little in the way of job redefinition. After the strike was settled, interviewers asked rank-and-file workers why they struck and whether or not they were satisfied with the company's settlement. With few exceptions, workers responded that they had struck for better pay and earlier retirement. Almost no one mentioned inhuman jobs. Asked what would make the settlement even better, workers responded, "higher pay and better retirement benefits."

In order to have stuck to their original intention, bargaining agents for the auto workers needed a better understanding of the assumptions underlying the auto workers' current relationship with their jobs and how these related to the nature and ideals of the workers. Before the strike, their pay was already considered fairly high. In performing inhuman jobs, the auto workers were behaving as if "There's no job too dirty to perform if the pay is high enough." By demanding more human jobs, the auto workers were acting *as if* "We want to be true to our ideals by working on meaningful tasks." But the bargaining agents apparently lost sight of the conflict between these assumptions and wound up negotiating a settlement that added another link to the chain that shackled workers to the assembly line. Moreover, the settlement made it unlikely that these workers would strike for better jobs in the immediate future. After all, how often can a person absorb the energy drain and financial sacrifice of a strike?

Alternatives

We have seen in Chapter 5 how choices offered by the organization do not pose real alternatives until we determine whether or not the options we're considering are based on different assumptions about our nature and our ideals. For the auto workers, a real alternative might have consisted of a choice between a pay raise and more human jobs. We also have seen that an alternative action differs from current practices by being based on assumptions that better approximate our unadapted nature and ideals. Now that we've familiarized ourselves with techniques for learning about our nature and exposing assumptions that explain how we've been operating in the organization, we can turn our attention to formulating alternatives. This is what produces the real opportunities for freedom in organization life.

Better alternatives seldom occur to us out of thin air. Usually, they are formulated after we recognize the inconsistencies between the assumptions that currently motivate us and those that more accurately reflect our nature and ideals. Some of the alternatives will necessitate changing the organization system and some will necessitate changing the type of relationship we form with the system. The larger the inconsistency, the easier it becomes to envision alternatives.

Regardless of which type of alternative we're considering, any improvements we can imagine are limited by our present comprehension of distorted self-pictures, illusions, and marginal understanding of ourselves and the system. In fact, we should interpret our inability to conceive of simple improvements for enhancing the quality of our organization life as an indication that we need to back up a step and go through another period of disciplined consciousness-raising.

Our ability to formulate alternatives depends on our having pursued a single aspect of organization life through each stage of the consciousness-raising model, remembering that the accomplishments at each stage become the input for the next. We're now at a point where we can develop more confidence in our grasp of this model by following an example through each stage of consciousness-raising.

Example

The following experiment was carried out by a group of European engineers and their wives. It grew out of their distress and sense of helplessness over the personnel practices that governed relocations to company headquarters in the United States. At the end of the experiment, they were asserting themselves and suggesting improvements of a quality seldom expressed at their company level.

Each of the thirteen engineers involved was beginning a one and a half to two year training assignment in the United States, spoke English, and were men. Most had first- or second-level supervisory experience. All were married. Their ages ranged from thirty to forty-five, and they had between three and twenty-five years experience with the company. The typical person was about thirty-three, had been with the company five years, and had two children. Initially, these engineers met to discuss adjustment problems created by their recent transfer. But when they became familiar with the consciousness-raising process, they decided to expand the scope of their discussions. They began meeting regularly, one entire day a month, and went on meeting for a year and a half.

As we have learned, the first stage of consciousness-raising uses feelings of incoherence to identify discrepancies, and this requires support and time for catharsis. In this instance, the engineers needed to overcome a feeling that "If I were just a little more adequate, I wouldn't have all these adjustment problems." They also needed time to release pent-up feelings of anger and frustration over the specific problems they'd been experiencing.

There was resentment with the company in general, and early discussions revealed problems and discrepancies in nearly every aspect of their work life. Some engineers complained that they had not been consulted when the transfer was planned for them, and some felt that not knowing the career consequences of turning it down forced them to move at inconvenient times for their family. Some resented that their wives were expected to leave good jobs without permits to work in the United States.

There was also resentment with the personnel department, which was charged with helping families relocate. The engineers complained that the neighborhoods chosen for their relocation suited the company's image rather than their own styles and preferences; that unfair policies dictated what they were allowed to ship at company expense; and that they had lost money as a result of the compensation formula that was supposed to provide them with a standard of living comparable with what they had in Europe and commensurate with what people in the United States earn for performing similar jobs.

There was resentment against the departments to which they had been reassigned. Some complained of bosses who were only understanding of relocation pressures as long as they put in a productive eight-hour day. Some complained that their expertise was disregarded because U.S. engineering practices were considered the best in the world.

The engineers resented their families because they were expected to make friends for their wives and were held accountable for problems that their children encountered at school. Some complained that their families treated the U.S. assignment as if it were a long vacation and were putting pressures on them to sightsee on weekends, when they needed time to rest and recoup from the pressures of the week.

The engineers resented the managers who made the decisions for international relocations. They didn't like the idea that they were considered part of a mobile work force that could be picked up and moved every few years. Some felt misled by the promises of rapid advancement that had been made when they were hired.

Overall, each of the engineers seemed to be suffering the pains of culture shock, because even the smallest problems seemed to be causing them high levels of concern and anxiety. Moreover, although each engineer complained of something different, listening to one another's complaints caused them to realize that various problems had similar causes.

The engineers soon realized that for their support group to be complete their wives would have to be included. Not only were the women deeply affected by relocation pressures but they were an essential part of the family's resources for coping with adjustment problems. At the end of the second meeting, the men decided to expand their group to include their wives. This type of unprecedented involvement in company matters, however, seemed to present additional adjustment pressures for two wives, and they declined to participate.

Once a list of discrepancies was identified, the group could turn their attention to the second stage of the consciousness-raising model. A period of divergent analysis produced many insights and clarifications about the actual workings of the organization system. The engineers insights included discovering that they believed that the company knew what's best for them; that they were afraid to turn down a transfer; that they were excessively dependent on the advice they get from higher level managers; that they felt the technical expertise they had developed in Europe was damn good and often superior to the methods used in the United States; that the longer they work for the company, becoming more technically specialized, the less desirable they become on the open job market; that being transferred caused them to feel insecure and marginal, like a guest who should follow the customs of his host; and that, in general, they didn't have the information they needed to manage their organization life intelligently.

Divergent analysis clarified their view of the organization system. The engineers discovered that policies regarding transfer allowances and compensation were not open for discussion, despite the image the personnel department tried to create; that people were controlled by never being sure of the consequences of saying no to a managerial request; that while people were encouraged to explore differences openly, they had better not be caught differing with their bosses in public; that a fail-safe system was emphasized, where the rewards for being right were seldom high enough to offset the punishments for being wrong; that they couldn't count on self-perspectives being solicited or considered when decisions were made about them; that families were treated as if they were mere appendages to the husband; and that the company's desire to put forth a conservative image often invaded their personal lives.

Strengthened by the divergent analysis of discrepancies, the engineers and their wives decided to collect some additional information about the actual way the system works and the assumptions made about them. They focused on the transfer process, because it was the primary source

119

of their current anxieties, and on the personnel department that administered these transfers. They decided to interview a representative sampling of those involved in transfer decisions. In order to cover themselves organizationally, they advised the personnel director of their plan. Because they were not asking for his permission, it would have taken more energy than it was worth for him to object.

The engineers and their wives were surprised at the results of their interviews. They discovered that despite the reassurances that management gave them about the transfer process, their feelings of uneasiness were well founded. Before a transfer was offered, the proposed move was passed up the line, level by level, to a vice-president. If blessed by him, the word went out to the personnel department, which asked the man about his interests. By this time, all managers concerned with the man's career are convinced that the transfer is a good idea. If the man refuses, the reasons for his refusal go back up the line to "a very disappointed" vice-president. The engineers concluded that it's misleading to assume that an immediate supervisor, representative of the personnel department, or any other company manager can present them with even-handed advice. They realized that each person in this chain had to answer many questions if a proposed transfer was refused.

Most families felt that they were not advised about all the benefits that were due them. The interviews determined, contrary to some of their suspicions, that the personnel department was not getting cost-effectiveness credit for saving money on unused transfer allowances. While personnel representatives didn't tell people about all the benefits to which they were entitled, they did this out of fear that a superior might come down hard on them if the company were exploited by a transferring family. As the personnel director frankly admitted, "Most line managers, as well as myself, have a tendency to formulate policies that protect against the two percent who are inclined to test the rules. I guess we sometimes overprotect the company."

Many other realizations crystallized as group members discussed what they had learned from their interviews. However, the main point was established: the engineers and their wives obtained perspectives that added to what they were able to induce from their own experience. Combined with what they had formerly realized, they were able to construct a better picture of the assumptions made about them and the actual way the organization worked. The fact that they chose to investigate transfers is secondary to the fact that they investigated an organization process.

120

Combining the information received from facing feelings of incoherence, identifying discrepancies, using divergent analysis, and interviewing others gave the engineers and their wives a more realistic picture of their relationships to the organization. At this point, they were involved in the third stage of consciousness-raising, and they began to comprehend more fully the vulnerabilities and costs involved in paternalistic liaisons like the ones they had formed with the company. They had traded understanding themselves and the organization for promises of protection and security. They discovered that company terms like career track, maturing process, and professional development were cover-ups for moving people around to meet corporate needs. Recognizing that transfers were motivated at least as much by company needs as by their own needs for training and development, they learned what they needed to know to make demands and to direct company resources toward their own personal and professional objectives. If a so-called training assignment was not teaching them much, they realized it was their responsibility to make the trade-off more equitable. Consciousness-raising was exposing assumptions that blocked the self-management of their lives.

The engineers and their wives were also surprised to discover that the more they learned about how the system worked, and the assumptions made about the people who comprise the system, the fewer villains they found. Increased knowledge led them to realize that no one was doing them in intentionally. For example, they could no longer reason that the personnel department was simply trying to make their own jobs easier at the expense of transferring families. If anything, the personnel department was in a worse box, for they were expected to have an answer for every question, and their answers were supposed to be consistent with any number of company policies built on erroneous and inconsistent assumptions about the human qualities of the people involved.

While each stage of consciousness-raising had its own immediate effects, providing the engineers and wives with increasingly accurate pictures of reality, there was a bigger payoff. This came in the fourth stage of consciousness-raising, when they used what they had learned to envision alternatives. Among the specific problems that transferring families had with personnel procedures was the almost inconsequential one in which a family of music buffs was refused an allowance to ship some records to the United States. The family reasoned that because they had not used two of their three-crate allowance for books, they were entitled to ship at least two crates of records. The personnel representative handling this request reasoned that this was not possible, because if he granted them permission to do this, others would demand the right to ship records in addition to books.

At first glance, it seemed like this couple was making a big deal out of nothing. Someone else might reason, "The hell with personnel. I'll ship the records at my own expense and tack on an extra twenty dollar cab fare to my moving expenses." But to this couple, their problem seemed to hold symbolic importance, although they couldn't initially figure out why. In fact, when I first asked them why it was so important, they looked sheepish and self-doubting.

But as the consciousness-raising progressed, their problem became the group's rallying point, and when its meaning and solution became evident, the group's sign of success. Wrapped up in this problem were all the assumptions an organization system makes when treating workers like children. Only if you assume you are a child, can you, as a matter of course, think of asking permission for something as inconsequential as substituting records for books. When the group discovered that the company leaders and the personnel director really intended to make transfers as easy as possible without much concern for costs, they were able to see numerous problems stemming from the same kind of discrepancy.

As the engineers and their wives discovered more about themselves, they learned that they often chided and complained like kids who don't get their way or when they felt trapped by a seemingly irrational company policy. The consciousness-raising process eventually led them to see that the entire transfer process was built on assumptions that they were children who must be monitored and closely supervised. The incident about the records would never have taken place if the existing procedure did not begin by telling people what they were entitled to take.

Envisioning alternatives became a relatively easy task once the group spotted inconsistencies between the organization's assumptions and expectations and what they believed to be their true nature. Until they discovered this difference in assumptions, each of their counterproposals merely perpetuated their dependence. Once they were able to articulate that they'd like to be treated like adults, it was relatively easy for them to envision alternatives. If prior to consciousness-raising someone had asked the engineers whether or not they were being treated and acted like adults, I'd guess only a few would have noticed that they were not. The tendency to believe that we are like our ideals is one of the most troublesome barriers to envisioning alternatives to current practices.

Reflection

In contrast to the pictures of reality acquired during socialization, the process of envisioning alternatives is mainly conscious, compatible with self-interests, and based on the lessons of our own experience. This time around, we shape our own reality, and if we get in trouble with the system, we'll have to take our lumps. But the lumps we take replace the lumps we've been taking all along without knowing it.

Newly envisioned alternatives stimulate an inner need either to change the organization system or to renegotiate our relationship with it. If the system fails to change or is intolerant of the changes we want to make, then we have a decision to make. At the extremes, we can either leave or live in discontent. Ultimately, no system is ideal for all the people who live in it. Some adaptation is always necessary; that's the nature of man's social contract. We'll have to reach our decision to stay or leave by weighing our priorities for change against our alternatives outside the organization. But we also must realize there is no Camelot; certain compromises are always necessary, and explicating our compromises allows us to take responsibility for our organization life.

Deciding whether or not there's a match between the alternatives we formulate and the goals of the system is a crucial step. We must not waste time deluding ourselves that we can make irreconcilables fit. We must know when we can modify our proposal in a way that makes no appreciable difference to us. This relies on our developing a thorough knowledge of the actual system. And, of course, we must also see when there's a ready fit. For example, the engineers and their wives formally proposed that personnel change their policies to treat them like responsible adults. They suggested that personnel ask transferring families what they need to take and what assistance they might like to have in making their transfer comfortable. Then if a request seemed excessive, the personnel representative could inquire further. A task force set up to consider their suggestion recommended that it be embodied in an experiment. Management expects this experiment to save the company money by people no longer shipping things they're entitled to, but don't particularly need, by reduced managerial aggravation, and by quicker adjustments to a new culture for the families involved. And the families are getting what they want: more control and autonomy in their relocation.

Even in instances such as the above, where benefits to the organization are readily apparent, there may be resistance. This is due to people with power assuming that each small step we take toward greater freedom and self-management means less control for them. They may not fear the particular step being negotiated as much as the step we'll want to take next. Chapter 19 will have more to say about the impact of our freedom on others. But the focus next is on what we need to know to make this fourth stage of consciousness-raising operational.

CHAPTER 18

Group Support for Stage 4

We are now at the stage of consciousness-raising where alternatives are formulated. Alternatives occur to us when we identify *inconsistencies* between assumptions that currently direct our organization life and assumptions that better approximate our nature. And nothing brings out the uncompromising purist in us more than a newly envisioned alternative. We usually want to act before we've considered the full range of alternatives. The challenge is to see whether or not our self-interests can fit within the parameters of change that our organization will tolerate.

Focusing on inconsistencies between assumptions, rather than focusing only on assumptions that reflect our nature, provides a contrast that stimulates thought about what would constitute a better situation; it gives us alternatives. Remember that there are two ways to make improvements in our organization life. First, we can propose changes in the way the organization works, and second, we can change our relationship with the organization. If we propose changes in the way the organization works, our proposal may be as specific as a single procedure or as widesweeping as a new policy or revamped organizational goals. However, specific procedures are manifestations of organization policies, and progress in changing them is likely to imply broad-reaching change. For example, one of the first changes considered by the transferring engineers was procedural, modifying the three-box limit for books to include records. But it didn't take long for them to see the underlying issue and recommend a new policy of self-managed transfers.

The second alternative, changing one's relationship to the organization, seems to be the easiest form to accomplish. At first, it seems as if we're the only ones involved. We feel it's easiest for us to change ourselves, and if we can't, what right do we have demanding that others reorder their lives to suit us? However, there are limits to just how much we can change without deeply affecting others. For example, we may decide to ask our subordinates for their evaluation of us. From our way of thinking, this seems like a good way to improve our managerial skills. From their way of thinking, it may be just one more double bind with which to cope. Here they are wanting to appear sufficiently competent to warrant a promotion, and we're trying to get them into an explicit discussion that will no doubt touch on some of the supervisory problems they pose for us.

Changing our relationship with one part of the organization system implies that we can do the same with other parts. For example, most of the engineers who had participated in the consciousness-raising experiment began redefining their interactions elsewhere in the company. One man decided that the company's policy regarding capital expenditures for improving manufacturing facilities was antiquated and illogical, and he set about changing it. The type of change he had in mind would require new types of relationships among high-level managers in engineering, manufacturing, and accounting.

Eventually, an entire group may try to change the organization. The probability of this happening is heightened when all group members are from the same organization and when most of them experience a prominent aspect of organizational life as unnatural. But such an effort requires a strategy, and this will be considered at length in the next chapter.

The Group Process

Hopefully, by the time a group has gotten this far, members will have worked out an effective style for interacting and will have confidence that they can invent procedures as they go along. In addition, they will need to agree on specific goals so that they can proceed with a common expectation of what they're trying to accomplish.

This is the stage in which the group has its last chance to counsel us before we finally put what we've learned into action. After much divergent reasoning, it's time for convergent problem-solving. We need to establish personal priorities and make decisions about how to pursue individual goals. Alternatives must be weighed and decisions made about how essential self-expression is to our life in the organization. In order for other group members to help, we'll need to fill out their picture of us. No doubt, conversations at previous stages have already provided them a fair perspective on our lives. But they will require even more specifics before they can start making valid suggestions for the decisions we now need to make. For instance, without knowing the importance someone places on remaining geographically near to his extended family, it's impossible to appreciate the factors inhibiting that person from asserting himself in a sensitive area and possibly risking his job.

Life stories are complicated and endless, and we can't tell everything. Nevertheless, there's much we can tell in the course of an hour by addressing ourselves to the essentials. We need to acquaint others with background information that helps them understand why the inconsistencies on which we intend to act are so filled with emotion. For instance, if we're particularly upset about an unjust promotion system, what should group members know to appreciate our special attachment to fairness or achievement. We'll find that others can follow us most easily when we proceed chronologically and by first describing an event and then explaining its significance. A period of questions and answers will also help. Of course, people can always get additional background later on when they sense in our resistance that something essential is missing in their understanding of us.

Once these perspectives on our life are filled out, we can get on with clarifying how misassumptions about our nature have affected our life in the organization. The clearer we are about how these assumptions are inconsistent with our nature, the easier we'll be able to envision alternatives. When inconsistencies are sharply stated and seem to apply to many group members, we can expect the discussion to flow smoothly. But when they are subtle or not obvious to others, the discussion is likely to be strained. This happens when someone gets wind of an inconsistency before everyone he thinks is affected by it sees its relevance, or when several group members think they've spotted an inconsistency that applies to a particular person before that person spots it himself. In such instances, the scene is set for confrontation. Someone may be prompted to say, "I think all of you guys have been taken in by this first-name baloney. We still work in a very status-oriented organization." On the other hand, he can always decide to let others live with their delusions. But if he does, a possibly important lesson is lost.

As we progress in consciousness-raising, interpersonal confrontation becomes less and less avoidable. By this stage, actions are being planned, and people realize that it takes a long time to undo the consequences of a misdirected act. Sometimes someone thinks, "I've got to stop him, even if it means he'll wind up resenting me." Although this type of reasoning usually comes out of a deep sense of concern, rather than a need to control, few actions produce consequences that can never be undone. When I believe a mistake might be costly, but not irreversible, I do my damnedest to make my point, but try not to impair my communications with the other person or leave him feeling that I've withdrawn my support. I want him to realize that while I strongly disagree with what he's proposing he can count on my being around if he later needs to pick up the pieces and start again.

Confrontations can be stressful when someone asks for advice that we can't give him. This is particularly likely on issues of life priorities and values, where it seems obvious that no one but the person involved can make the decision. In such instances, the struggle is likely to be implicit and the confrontation covert. We find ourselves fighting with the unstated, guilt-provoking message: "If you really care about me, you would at least tell me what you would do in the same circumstance." In such instances, we can get bloodied talking about the other person's dependency, but we might not come out too badly by talking about our own dilemma in wanting to help but not having a sufficient perspective on that person's life to offer intelligent advice. By this time, I hope you realize that I'm not opposed to facing conflict explicitly; I'm just opposed to conflict that doesn't raise consciousness or that weakens the supportive components of our relationships.

Work at this stage of consciousness-raising is time-consuming. It takes time to clarify inconsistencies, probe the ramifications of specific alternatives, modify alternatives that seem impractical, and expand the range of alternatives being considered. Some topics will need repeated attention until group members figure out an approach that seems practical. Moreover, ideas formulated at one meeting will get confused during the course of the workweek, decisions to take action will reap unexpected reactions, and experience in trying to change one aspect of organization life will create opportunities in other areas.

Just because our support group has performed work at each of the three preceding stages of consciousness-raising, we cannot assume that we have acquired all the perspectives needed to formulate alternatives. Once an inconsistency becomes blatant, alternatives will quickly occur to us. But most of the time, group discussions will be monopolized by inconsistencies on which members have yet to focus properly. Thus, when our group finds itself belaboring a particular inconsistency, having little success formulating alternatives, it is likely that we're at a point where we need to recycle. This means taking the same area of concern and identifying more feelings of incoherence, going through another period of divergent analysis, and perhaps performing additional reconnaissance into organizational perspectives.

Listening to alternatives proposed by other support group members presents us with some obvious opportunities to help. First, we can substantiate that another person has based his proposal on an accurate picture of the facts, as established in prior group discussions. Second, we can monitor the logic of what's being formulated. Third, we can broaden the range of alternatives being considered by chiming in with additional alternatives and, in particular, by challenging him to go the other way. That is, if his alternatives seem to center around directly changing the organization, we can help him consider changing his relationship to the organization.

Listening to someone else's proposals often stimulates an impulse to give advice. Giving advice in a support group is a necessary but sticky function. We'll continually be surprised by how often someone passes up the most obvious alternatives. Each person predictably blocks out certain alternatives, and no doubt, he'll learn about some of these during consciousness-raising. But the unconscious is so complicated and expansive that one can never hope to take complete control. Besides, even if a person could, he'd lose some of the fun in living.

Any suggestions that we make should be put in the pool of things the other person is considering. When our advice gets heard as an expert's prescription, the person receiving it is in danger of trading one type of dependent condition for another. Thus, we need to be on the alert for support group members asking us what they should do before they have an adequate chance to think things through for themselves. Situations where others defer too much to our advice should be handled delicately. We need to get the other person back in the director's role, perhaps by statements like, "Perhaps we're running ahead of ourselves," or "I'm confused and maybe we ought to go back and examine the assumptions on which we've been proceeding." Something more direct can cause the other person to overreact and refrain from asking about our perspectives.

As we raise consciousness at this fourth stage of the model, we develop elaborate perspectives on one another's lives and aspirations, and defenses. We learn to trust one another and develop empathy for another person's struggle. Even the smallest personal gains will engender our appreciation because we understand what they symbolize in the life of the person involved, and what they predict for the future. This type of appreciation is hard to come by in our society and tends to bind us together. So it's no surprise that support groups have a tendency to continue meeting beyond the time of peak efficiency and productivity.

I would never advise a support group to break up just because their productivity peaked. Emotional support and feelings of goodwill may be the ultimate products that a support group creates. However, I am against a support group prolonging its meetings without members realizing why and without their explicating the change in their group's purpose. Gaining control of organization life is a neverending battle that must be faced, despite the fact that each of us gets battle weary. So perhaps we'll decide to continue our support group indefinitely, but after a while, we might also consider joining an additional group.

Each person has is own natural rhythm for raising consciousness, and periodic respites are necessary. Don't forget how the images that originally characterized our adaptations to the organization system lulled us into thinking that we were free. Conversely, a support group, in which we experience loving care and escape the tensions of the outside world, can become the ultimate in mantraps, because we can be lulled into neglecting our interests in worldly projects. In my mind, this trap fosters many of the elements of complacency to which George, the man who retired on the job, succumbed in his organization life. We must be careful that we don't retire too early from the job of exerting control over our organization lives.

Reflection

Changing our relationship with the organization is an indirect way of changing the way the organization works. As we change, higher-level managers have to change their way of dealing with us. It's analogous to the ways certain tools would have to be redesigned if the majority of people were left-handed. If many of us were aware of our nature and the actual way the organization worked, then incentives used to motivate us, the communication system, and the way we're evaluated would change. And they already do this to some extent. For instance, each of us has had the experience of being asked for our opinions when the person has the authority and desire to make the decision on his own. He seeks our advice because he realizes that he can't implement the project without our being involved.

While redefining our relationship with the organization is an energy-draining process, it's much easier for us when the organization changes. Then we can redirect our efforts to getting other aspects of organization life to better reflect our nature. However, the particular strategy we use for getting an organization to change is touchy business. When we try to change others, we run the risk of inciting counterforces that can distort our projects and set our efforts back years. Developing a noninflammatory strategy for changing the organization system is the topic of the next chapter.

CHAPTER 19

Stage 5: Affecting the Organization Life of Others

There's no getting around it. Increasing control over our organization life ultimately depends on the organization changing. I know that thus far I've given the impression that gaining control is mainly a matter of expanded consciousness rather than deliberately changing the organization. However, each time we successfully put an alternative into action, we automatically expand our capacity for envisioning even better ones. Consciousness, and the control it brings, is developed through successive approximations. Improvements act to consolidate our gains and support our next thrust.

Whether we're trying to change the organization directly or to redefine our relationship to it, we eventually reach a point where we need to engage people outside our support group. There are many reasons for this. First of all, people on other levels and with different roles possess pictures of reality based on their own experiences that, when comprehended by us, help us upgrade and expand our own formulations of reality.

Second, unless others also become more free, our own increased freedom will merely replace one form of elitism with another. Our reasons for wanting to avoid elitism are practical as well as ideological. We must not make our raised consciousness the basis of a new competitive system in which the have-nots fantasize more about how they can take it away from the haves than they think about how everyone can have more.

Third, "they'll" never let us make it without them. Even in the most permissive organizations, people reach a limit in their tolerance for nonconformity and idiosyncratic expression, (which is how our renegotiated relationships with the organization will appear to the uninvolved). And when they reach that limit, they will become reactionary. In fact, if I can generalize from my experience, the further one gets without meeting opposition, the more severe will be the counterforces that eventually appear.

And, fourth, the job is too big for us to handle by ourselves. Other people, pooling the lessons of their experience with what they can learn from others, including ourselves, will make gains that effect everyone. Religion and humanistic psychology repeatedly demonstrate that when people are in touch with their actual nature and their ideals, their chances of acting collaboratively, benevolently, even lovingly toward others are greatly increased. Organization science needs to exploit this lesson.

Top-down Change Doesn't Make It

In a large company in which I once did some consulting, managers joke about the golden wave of change. The golden wave refers to the periodic introduction of programs that simultaneously address problems of organization effectiveness and human well-being. The joke is based on their understanding that no fundamental change is going to take place and that the smart manager ducks his head long enough to let the newest wave of change crest above him. Fifteen years ago, the golden wave was systems analysis; ten years ago, it was management by objectives; five years ago, it was organization development; and today it is social audits and programs in minority awareness.

Because golden waves are typically initiated from the top, people feel it's best not to oppose them. Co-opting the organization is probably the cagiest way of escaping them. People who are good at this are among the first to learn about a new program, use its buzzwords, and exploit its principles in a controlled work situation. At the conscious level, these people seem to be sincere in experimenting with the methods, and genuine in attempting to improve their work life. But something inside them resists. When the going gets rough and they have to choose between old ways and new, they rely on the old. The overall effect is that people do better at talking about and experimenting with the methods of a particular program than actually changing anything fundamental in the way they conduct their organization life.

While there is no one reason that explains exactly why people resist, there are times when their resistance is most likely to be expressed, usually at the point where others, besides top management, are expected to initiate improvements. Each of the above mentioned programs begins with a top-down strategy for change. Of course, it is intended that once the principles are grasped by people at all levels of the organization the strategy will shift and improvements will be initiated by each level. Eventually, people at various levels are expected to stop waiting around for managerial directives that specify which changes will be made and how. Each person is supposed to reflect on the techniques he's learned and initiate changes toward increased work effectiveness and increased job satisfaction. And in being an initiator, a person experiences new autonomy that is supposed to be an added job satisfaction.

However, the procedure for change inevitably bogs down when it is time for others besides top management to initiate. Upper management begins withholding information that others need if they are to comprehend their work situation well enough to make proposals that are practical, and lower levels begin feeling uptight about possibly overstepping their domain of responsibility and being penalized. The overall result is the same. Organization members at all levels reach a point where they contend that they've extracted the major benefits of the approach and that it's time to turn their energy toward new ways of enhancing the managerial process. Let me illustrate with two examples from my consulting work. One involves an upper-management group who twice aborted their program when on the brink of opening themselves to proposals from below, and the other involves people at lower organization levels who backed away and hid when offered a chance to publicly discuss changes that they thought would improve their organization.

Example 1

This example involved the six-member, top-management team of the research and development division within a reasonably large company. The division was made up of about one hundred scientists, seventy-five laboratory technicians, and twenty-five secretaries. Their job was to develop new products and upgrade existing ones. I began by interviewing members to find out the issues they thought stood between them and better management of the division. A number of interpersonal conflicts and knotty work problems were identified, and we began to have team-building meetings aimed at improving communications and problem-solving effectiveness. At this time, comparable consultation was conducted within most of the other work teams in the division. The top group progressed rapidly, and after a year and a half, I found them cohesive, relatively noncompetitive, and willing to work collaboratively on potentially conflictive issues like assigning people to projects and preparing the division's budget. Cohesiveness and interdependence progressed to where team members could directly discuss how to get more enjoyment out of their work and how to form closer ties with one another.

The crunch for this top-management team came when, over the course of several meetings, they had crystallized their ideal plan for managing the division, but couldn't implement the next step. Their plan was a progressive one that encouraged individuals at all levels to assume project initiation and leadership. The plan was written up into a working paper that they wanted to circulate for comments prior to implementation, but I made a case for first asking other groups throughout the division to develop ideal plans of their own. Afterward, a series of meetings could be scheduled in which groups would exchange their statements and discuss differences. In my concept, these meetings would have a divergent focus with people asking, "What do our differences tell us about ourselves and about how our division has been operating?" They agreed to try it this way.

However, the top-management group reneged on their agreement. They reasoned, "Let's not trick the lower levels. Let's show them our statement first and *then* ask them to develop their own." As might have been expected, no substantive revisions were suggested by the lower levels. Even without additional ideas, the changes implied by top management's plan seemed to pay off. People at each organizational level broadened the scope of their activities and organization interests. But an important opportunity was lost. By refusing to challenge lower organizational levels to *openly* think for themselves, management lost the chance to have their thinking enhanced, and lower levels lost the opportunity to exercise real influence.

There's an interesting postscript to this story. About a year later, a second colleague conducted an independent survey of reactions to the changes that were taking place. He wrote a thorough report that was mainly positive, but revealed discrepancies in how various organizational levels perceived one another as well as how they perceived the changes. Again, I thought that much could be accomplished by letting everyone in the organization see the report and use it to spark discussions in various ad hoc as well as formal groupings. There was paternalism in my suggestion, because I made it only after concluding that there wasn't much in the report that could cause people aggravation. I thought the report would stimulate people at every level to think about their position and role in the organization, and provide something tangible to use in having discussions with those who see things differently. This time, however, my proposal was voted down directly. Members of the top-management team could not see much advantage in letting people react to the report without their control. They favored giving it to the next level down and seeing whether or not that group wanted to show it to the people who reported to them. After all, this top-management group reasoned, "We don't want to undermine the authority of the managers who report to us."

Example 2

The next example of people's resistance to breaking the top-down chain of control involves a strategy developed by an upper-management team and endorsed by a representative sample of their organization. This strategy also broke down when its implementation got to the stage where lower levels were supposed to initiate change.

In many respects, this organization was similar to the one in the preceding example. After about a year of assisting managers at various levels to work together more effectively, I proposed that a task force, with representation from each organization level, be formed and charged with identifying opportunities for improving and changing the organization. Top management agreed, and such a group was formed, with me as their consultant. We met on a monthly basis, each time with a different work group minus their boss. We listened to people's problems and ideas for improvements. As a rule of thumb, we would not directly intervene on someone's behalf. We tried to confine ourselves to giving suggestions about what people could do to improve things themselves. We listened, reacted, and encouraged others in the work group to contribute their ideas and support one another.

In rare instances, we volunteered direct help. For example, we offered to arbitrate a conflict between a man and his supervisor, but only after the man himself tried to work out his problems more directly. Although our meetings were confidential, we planned to send out a monthly bulletin describing, in general terms, issues we encountered and suggestions we made that seemed to have relevance beyond the work group involved.

Our format lasted only three months, and our accomplishments left something to be desired. After meeting with the accounting managers I described near the beginning of Chapter 4, we suggested that they form a task force to deal with their career problems. This eventually led to their list of mealymouthed suggestions that were dismissed by top management.

We met with a group of secretaries and listened to their feelings of being underutilized. We proposed that they initiate a course to teach their bosses how to draw more fully on their resources. The course was designed to be fun as well as informative, was scheduled for the *five minutes* preceding each Friday morning coffee break, and each week would be conducted by different secretaries. The invitations went out for the first session for which the entire group planned the curriculum. A few bosses balked at first, but eventually everyone accepted. The first week's course was cancelled when an organization crisis arose, and it was never rescheduled.

The organization's support for our task force collapsed when we interviewed a group of first-level managers, and their bosses started acting paranoid. They peeked in the glass window of our meeting room, buttonholed lower status members of our committee, and generally attempted to set the record straight, even though they had no idea of what we were discussing. They acted as if our group was evaluating them instead of supporting people to work out their own problems and improve the organization. And so our task force was defeated. We disbanded without even publishing the first issue of our bulletin.

Reflection

On the basis of many consulting experiences, I've become wary of the type of self-management and autonomy that occurs once a top-down change process has been initiated. I'm still working on several projects in which we're hoping that perspectives developed at top organizational levels will stimulate and support increased consciousness and self-management by lower levels. But I'd work differently if organizations were more egalitarian and open. I've seen better results when consciousness-raising among middle- and lower-level groups begins without a pre-established plan for working through channels. Such was the case with the European engineers described in Chapter 17.

The basic problem in catalyzing self-management within the middle and lower levels lies in getting people the information they need to build a more comprehensive picture of reality and the support they need to act on it. As the two preceding examples illustrate, I've encountered resistance at every organizational level. The reasons for this resistance vary by level, even though the outcomes are the same. Top management cloaks its perspectives because it feels that wide-scale dissemination would create disagreement and conflict that in turn would lead to an undisciplined and chaotic organization. Upper-middle management hides its perspectives because it feels that the managerial power of those below them would be eroded, creating stresses that those middle managers cannot control. Middle managers conceal their perspectives because they fear that they'll create conflict that will be seen by those above them as a deficiency in their managerial skills. First- and second-level managers don't share their perspectives because they're not sure of what they know, and because they don't put much stock in the quality of discussions they're likely to provoke. And, finally, first-level staff and technicians don't search out higher level perspectives because either they're busy trying to demonstrate their loyalty and competence or they're trying to numb themselves to the pain of being so far out of control.

Developing a Strategy for Organization Change

Organization life is political and competitive. Many obvious improvements that we suggest will be dismissed for reasons that are unrelated to their substance. Furthermore, people don't readily admit using power-seeking tactics, even to themselves, and this makes the going all the trickier. Even in instances where we don't intend to compete or to control, others will impute these motivations to us. Moreover, we are human, with partially developed skills and unconscious influences, and our well-intended actions will often fall short of our ideals.

Developing a strategy for changing the organization becomes even more complicated when we realize that consciousness is also a political issue. Our increased consciousness will mean that those immediately above us in the organization will be threatened, in part, because they derive their security and power from being considered smarter than us and from being able to control our actions. Those below us will be threatened, in part, because they derive their security and power from being ready to step in and fill our shoes and from being able to anticipate our concerns. Even those adjacent to us will be threatened, in part, because they derive their security and power from having comparable skills to us and will be troubled by our relating to issues that aren't even in their field of focus. Perhaps the worst threat of all is the one we create for ourselves, if we think that our expanded scope gives us a substantially better perspective than ones held by others.

Rather than go through the painstaking procedures needed to change an organization, we might consider dropping out and creating a new one that doesn't have so many bad habits to overcome. However, this strategy too is not without its risks. While we can now see a multitude of inadequacies in the current system, part of the reason we can see them is because the system that has evolved deals with certain human issues successfully, and the structure has become stabilized. Most organizations represent more progress than we're aware of. Beginning a new organization puts us back to rediscovering fundamentals that are implicit and covered over in the present way of doing things. Encountering so many basic issues at once leads to compromises that are usually no better than the ones we're already living. The present organization system at least gives us something solid to brace against in developing leverage for a thrust toward greater personal freedom.

I've concluded that the success of any strategy for changing the organization through consciousness-raising depends on the extent to which that strategy involves and benefits others. Thus, I think the actions we take to help others eventually formulate their own ideas of what improvements need to be made are the real *products* of our expanded consciousness. In contrast, I think the changes in the system which are the direct result of our own insights are but the *by-products* of our consciousness-raising.

Thus, mine is a collaborative strategy in which we follow through on our insights with attempts to get other key people to reflect and develop insights of their own. As others become aware of the implications a particular discrepancy holds for their own humanity and effectiveness in the organization, they will be motivated to search more thoroughly for the lessons contained in their own experience. Once they are convinced that we're not going to steal prerogatives that are appropriately theirs, then they are likely to open themselves to the human lessons contained in their own experiences. A collaborative strategy like this has additional advantages for us. We avoid placing others in the position of merely evaluating *our* proposals, and we don't weaken our own positions by rendering others dependent on our ingenuity and willingness to act on their behalf.

A Statesmanlike Approach to Organization Change

I call the strategy I use the statesmanlike approach. It is based on a couple of simple assumptions that I've been making throughout this book. First, the same job can be accomplished effectively in any number of ways and might just as well be performed in a way that's consistent with the nature and ideals of the people involved instead of in a way that relies on role-determined behavior and tough-minded organization discipline. Second, organizations where enough people are engaged in developing a better connection to their own nature and a more realistic picture of the organization will operate more effectively than organizations where people are socialized to live with discrepancies.

I call this approach statesmanlike because it directs people to build up the organization by supporting others rather than by vying for partisan interests. It is also statesmanlike in that it encourages people at every level to contribute their ideas for organizationwide improvements. It's a particularly challenging approach because the people we're supporting are those we probably faulted when we went through our own consciousness-raising. Putting this approach into action requires resisting our inclination to overpersonalize our role in problems and miss the systemwide issues. This approach requires that we transcend our conditioning and view ourselves as the symptom not the cause of organizational problems.

Example 1

The tendency to overpersonalize a problem and not view its systemwide consequences is illustrated by what happened to a lawyer working for a posh law firm. Henry was in his late thirties, quite successful, going through the throes of a divorce, and questioning his values and his identity. Henry's searching took the form of experimenting with his image. One month, he grew a beard; the next month, he shaved it off. Then it was a sports car, a mustache, new clothes, frizzy hair, no mustache, a new apartment, and, finally, sporty dress without a necktie. This is when *they* went after him.

It seems there was a conflict over pay rates in his firm. Henry was one level below the top and earning something on the order of two hundred thousand dollars a year. Lawyers two levels down in the firm were upset about the pay differential that netted them an annual salary of one hundred twenty-five thousand dollars. They complained to the senior partners that they were underpaid, and they publicly criticized Henry for his unbusinesslike attitude, now exemplified by his sporty dress. One day, Henry was called into a meeting of the senior partners and told "We think you're making a mistake. We don't want to embarrass you, but these people are making you their target. The last thing in the world we want you to do is give up your personal freedom, but. . . ."

The senior partners never acknowledged to Henry, or even to one another, the real nature of the dissatisfaction. In everyone's mind, Henry was the irritant. And he was hurt by it. Ken, a friend of his, told me, "Henry hasn't been the same since. It tore me up as well. It was one of the few times when someone's hurt in the business world got to me. I've never felt the same about our firm since."

Each person who focused on Henry's sporty dress, including Henry, helped to cover over the fundamental problem. If Henry, the senior partners, or the rebellious lawyers could have focused on a divergent line of reasoning, the organization system might have been improved, and Henry could have been spared the hurt. Henry's friend added perspective: "I'm absolutely sure that all of us in the firm translate money into approval. If someone would just once come into my office and tell me 'I think you're doing a great job,' it would make all the difference in the world to me. I would work for half the pay. But we're all so fuckin' needy that no one's able to say it. In my wildest dreams, I never thought I'd be earning this much, but now I sit at my desk dreaming of more."

Ken went on to tell me his own story, which added even more perspective to the firm's real problem of which Henry was merely a symptom. After Ken had been in the firm three years, he was called in for a review. At this time, the senior partners expressed their disap-

141

pointment in his progress. A two-hour discussion boiled down to the fact that Ken was not bringing enough money into the firm. At the time, the firm had twenty-five lawyers and no office administrator. Ken had been spending part of his time coordinating office administration, running the firm's law school recruiting program, and getting involved in philosophical discussions on legal areas in which he was not directly working. After Ken got the word, he started to improve. He dropped administration and recruiting responsibilities, made it known that he was no longer available for ad hoc discussions—in fact he even stopped eating lunch—and launched himself full time into bringing money into the firm. He shifted his practice to the most lucrative area he could find and became successful. Today, he's a partner bringing in five times more income than his pay, and he has jumped over several others in the firm's pay hierarchy.

In the absence of colleague interaction, Ken and his fellow lawyers are in the same position. Each is reduced to evaluating his productivity and worth in terms of money. How much income would they sacrifice for other types of reward? It seems as if they easily could have the best of both worlds. But to reach a point where they could view their alternatives would require that someone like Henry refrain from personalizing an organization problem long enough to divergently analyze its systemwide meaning.

The statesmanlike approach entails understanding the perspectives of those who have key roles in problems created by discrepancies, finding out how they view an event or situation that signals a discrepancy to us, and discovering the function their viewpoints serve, both for them personally and for the organization. In the preceding example, as long as the senior partners viewed the flap about Henry's dress as competition within their ranks, they could avoid paying attention to their highly competitive relationships with one another and the affect these relationships had on subordinates. For instance, if the law firm continues with its present system, it's inevitable that the rebellious lawyers will be sniped at from the ranks below them.

Example 2

Another facet of the statesmanlike approach entails inquiring into other people's perspectives. Even when we think we've got a good fix on a situation that contains a discrepancy, we may find some surprises.

142

And our inquiry will help others see how they are personally connected to the discrepancy, which in turn generates additional support from them. As an example of how this is accomplished, let us consider again the case of the engineer, mentioned briefly in the preceding chapter, who decided to change his company's policy for improving manufacturing facilities.

The company this engineer worked for had no budget for in-plant improvements other than what was required to conform with safety and pollution codes. Expenditures for improved lighting, for replacing rather than repairing worn equipment, and for people-savers such as hydraulic lifts and air conditioning had to be bootlegged under the heading of lowering production costs, for which the company had an established procedure. Capital could be used as long as the expenditure was recouped from production savings within a period of 2.8 years.

Whenever an improvement was needed that did not directly reduce production costs, it was up to an engineer to come up with another proposal that could cut costs dramatically. Then the indirect and direct improvements would be lumped together in a single proposal that met the 2.8 year pay-back requirement. This method required a collusion between the manufacturing representative, the plant accountant, and Chuck, the engineer in this case. If the engineering estimate was off and it took more than 2.8 years to recoup the money expended, manufacturing was obliged to protect Chuck by finding another account, called a rathole, to hide the overage. While each person's boss was involved, no one knew just how far up the line the authorization for this madness stretched.

Chuck began his attempt to change this policy by convening a meeting with his manufacturing and accounting counterparts, calling their attention to this discrepancy, and describing the problems created for him by it. He asked them if this policy caused them problems. As he had hoped, the others expressed problems of their own, as well as a desire to get this policy changed, although they were skeptical that this could be accomplished. Chuck asked each of them to explain how he had learned to operate the way he did and what he thought this procedure accomplished for the organization. He suggested that in preparation for another meeting they interview their bosses to find out why the higher-ups endorsed this procedure and what problems it caused them. Chuck realized that higher-ups would need to be involved if the system were going to change. Eventually, a meeting was held between the three counterparts, their bosses, and the division manager.

Each had been involved in a number of divergent discussions prior to the meeting and thus had had a chance to consider the issues involved. They quickly decided that this discrepancy was a vestige of long-standing suspicions among top-management people who were no longer around. Like so much of what bothers us in our organization life, this procedure had taken on an existence all its own. It was begun for one reason, and people who never understood the original rationale invented their own reasons for keeping it going.

The statesmanlike approach proceeds the same way whether we're at an upper level trying to get perspectives and support from lower levels or whether we're at a lower level trying to get perspectives and support from above. The statesmanlike approach challenges upper-level managers to contribute their questions and uncertainties, and challenges lower-level personnel to forget their anxieties about specific concerns long enough to consider the systemwide issues of which their concerns are only symptoms.

Example 3

Overall, the statesmanlike approach encourages people at various levels of the organization to pool what they have learned from experience. Each person needs to contribute his own perspectives, open himself to perspectives held by others, and search for microcosms of his organization life in the struggle of others. Microcosms are the parallels that can be drawn between the problems and discrepancies with which we see others struggling and the yet unidentified discrepancies in our own organization life. Recognizing the microcosm introduces humility into the process of consciousness-raising. A recent personal experience is illustrative.

For years, doctoral students in my department at UCLA complained of feeling depressed upon learning they had passed their qualifying exams. Just when we all expected they'd feel like celebrating with champagne, they went out drinking beer to drown a depression. Neither I nor my colleagues could understand why. Then a student expressed his predicament in a way that not only helped me to understand his blues but to see a parallel in my own life at the university. It seems that when we tell students they have passed we also tell them about the weaknesses we see in their answers, and the limitations to intellectual rigor these weaknesses imply. Their feelings of success are undermined by faculty comments about their imperfections. We think we're using the exam as a diagnostic device; they think they're being criticized.

These insights revealed a parallel in the way faculty promotions are handled. We've always called our system the meat grinder, but never knew how to change it. No matter how much we've accomplished, worked, or learned, we're given an elaborate critique of our imperfections at the same time we're told we've been promoted.

Now we have a group of champagne-drinking students because we wait at least three weeks after we tell them they've passed to tell them the weak spots we've diagnosed while examining them. However, as you might have guessed, we've made little progress in changing the system of evaluating and giving feedback to our faculty.

Reflection

Ultimately, the statesmanlike approach has a domino effect in which each person's insights are used to stimulate the thinking of others. This effect is exemplified in the way the products and by-products of the statesmanlike approach are defined. The products are the consciousness and challenges in self-management we excite in others; The by-products are the consciousness and improvements we instill in our own organization life.

Very few people base their quest for freedom on the suppression and control of others. People resort to controlling and suppressing others when they sense that they have no control over their own life. As much as anything, the statesmanlike approach helps us focus on supporting those who are removed from learning the lessons of their daily experience and are not very much in control. Ultimately, exerting control over our own lives depends on their being in control of their lives.

CHAPTER 20

Group Support for Stage 5

Once we've decided the organization needs to change, how do we proceed? On the one hand, we can advocate a specific change, or on the other, we can open-endedly support other people's considerations. When we approach the organization with a specific alternative in mind, we are in the position of being an advocate of change. We seldom take this position unless we believe the alternative is one that will measurably improve the quality of organization life. It's typically an alternative in which we have confidence: one that's based on the lessons of our own experience and that has been modified to incorporate the ideas of others in our support group and the information collected by interviewing and observing key people in the organization. For example, the European engineers might want to propose a job-bidding procedure to replace a system that effects transfers with more concern for the job to be done than for who would like to do it.

We can also approach the organization open-endedly, supporting other people as they consider what needs to change. We bring a discrepancy to their attention, invite discussion on the overall problems caused by the discrepancy, and leave them alone to do what they want about it. In this approach, we define our role as one of assisting others to make responses that are more consistent with their own nature and ideals than the ones they've been making. For example, the European engineers might begin by calling attention to the discrepancies produced for higher-level managers when faced with the personnel problems involved in transferring lower-level people to different company locations. They would then open-endedly ask what could be done to form a better match between project needs and human desires.

146

The Statesmanlike Approach

The statesmanlike approach combines the advocate of change and the open-ended ways of proceeding. It gives us a way of remaining open to new ideas, even after we've formulated an alternative, without losing our focus when we encounter the perspectives of others.

The statesmanlike approach almost always entails our stimulating others to think divergently. However, it's important that we proceed open-endedly and let the other person's experience provide the subject matter for his reflections. Otherwise, they will find that *their* insights are the product of *our* experience. And in such instances, their freedom will lie in their eventual ability to oppose us.

When others think divergently, they become conceptual rather than emotional and thus find a new way of looking at their anxieties. But we'll have problems getting them to use their conceptual skills. In particular, we'll find ourselves wanting others to think divergently immediately after they've stated a problem, which is the very moment they are ready for convergent problem-solving. For instance, if the head of a federal agency was upset because of a 35 percent turnover rate, we would want him to stop his agonizing for a while to consider what this tells us about government work. Unless we meet his concerns head-on, however, our raising the divergent question will only increase his apprehension that the problem as he currently sees it might go unsolved. This would only further heighten his impulse to think convergently.

Thus, before asking the divergent question, it's important to relate as directly as we can to the current formulation of the problem. We know that his formulation of the problem is arbitrary: the same situation receives ten different labels from ten different people. It's obvious that he's focusing on morale; someone else might focus on job design. We also know that problems are frequently phrased in such a way that the solution is implied by the question. His problems would go away if the turnover rate dropped. If the turnover rate dropped, but agency effectiveness were not improved, the agency head would feel less anxious. Therefore, we might address his concerns by saying something like, "I see what you're getting at," and by mentioning the issue specifically, perhaps adding our own understanding of what's involved in *his* conceptualization of the problem. Then we would need to explain why we want him to reflect divergently. We could tell him that something more basic might result from studying the situation further. We might express our willingness to come back to his statement of the problem if we don't make headway. Now's our chance to formulate some questions that treat the problem as if it were a symptom of something more basic, and we tell him this is what we're going to do. We want our questioning to lead us to consider what his definition of the problem implies about himself, other people in the agency, the real workings of this agency, and the relationship federal workers have to government.

The statesmanlike approach makes us informal support group members for each person we contact. We can gain additional perspectives on what we're undertaking by remembering the time and energy it took to build rapport and understanding among members of our own group. But there's a limit to how much support we can provide informally; eventually, each person needs his own formal support group.

Supporting people on an informal basis produces many frustrations. In our society, it's fairly common to put down people who resist or block our statesmanlike efforts, particularly when we are benevolently motivated. It's also common to try to cement a new collaboration by criticizing a third person whose efforts are a hindrance both to us and the person we're trying to support. But let us assume the statesmanlike approach means resisting these tendencies toward criticism. If we're judgmental about someone who isn't present, the person we're with may begin to suspect we are equally critical behind his back. But we are bound to snipe occasionally, we don't want to put down ourselves, and we don't want to put down others who are critical when we're around. For example, a colleague whom I had been trying to support approached me recently with a crack about another member of our consulting team. I replied, "I'm trying not to do that anymore." He immediately got my message. It was simple. His feelings didn't appear hurt, and I tried not to come off holier than thou. My support group helped me to develop this attitude.

Although we may have no intention of this, attempting to change an organization carries the implicit threat that either things change or someone will quit. On the other hand, I'm not against someone quitting, particularly when he does so because the organization is not able to change fast enough on some dimension that is crucial to his identity. In fact, I'd even go so far as to state that I think a 10 percent annual quitting rate is desirable both for the organization and for the people

148

who have yet to quit. I know most organizations abhor this view. Some managers even go so far as to call those who leave defectors.

However, when we feel like quitting because the organization hasn't been sufficiently responsive to our activities for change, there are a couple of thoughts we ought to keep in mind. First, we need to remember that no organization changes instantly, and by using the statesmanlike approach, we're probably doing more to lay the ground-work for future change than we are to bring about immediate change. Second, and most important, more change may be taking place than we are aware of, and it may be that our preoccupation with a specific alternative makes us miss other improvements that are taking place. For instance, we might be concerned that minorities still have to work their way up through the promotion system, and miss the fact that interracial communication is loosening up. Support group members can help us see when our efforts are paying off.

Conversely, because we need to feel that our efforts are paying off, we are susceptible to accepting superficial changes without examining the depth of those changes. Here the support group can help us not to overestimate the change that's taken place. In such instances, we'll find it particularly useful to have people from outside our immediate work unit as members of our group.

In our discussion of the statesmanlike approach, the role of the support group so far has been more or less in the background. This is because once we start engaging other people in the organization our primary need is for backup support and perspective. Moreover, by the time our group has gotten this far, each member will have a pretty good idea of how he needs to operate. The only specific suggestion I can make is that the members periodically consider the merits of disband-ing and joining other groups. The relationships we've developed with members of our current group will naturally continue to be relevant to new problems we encounter. We can treat former support group members as friends we call on or meet with to exchange ideas when struggling with a knotty problem.

I've intentionally delayed commenting on what can be the most powerful tactic for changing an organization: banding together with our support group and trying to change some aspect of the organiza-tion. This is the riskiest type of action a support group can take. A group of similarly situated people can gain a hearing in almost any quarter of the organization merely by being serious, friendly, and articulate. On the other hand, acting as a group can spark reactionary forces that cause others to put down our proposals without a hearing. Even if just one person appears capricious, overly demanding, or too politically minded, our project can easily be scuttled and credibility lost for all the members of the support group.

I've often seen the kibosh put on an entire unit when an informal group with a cause appeared to overstep its boundaries or acted brazenly. Such was the case in 1970 when a group of middle-level managers attempted to hold a meeting after working hours in the company auditorium to protest the incursion of the United States into Cambodia. Not only were they denied the use of the auditorium but their division manager received a vicious dressing down from higher-ups for not being able to keep his people in line.

No group should take on an organization discrepancy as a group project without individual members first recognizing the basis of their motivations, arguing through their differences, and researching the pictures of reality held in other parts of the organization. We can never tease out the full complexity of other people's realities, but a comprehensive scanning can help us avoid obvious pitfalls. Recognizing that our view of another group's reality is never complete, means that we should probably err on the side of raising elementary questions in our open-ended approach to them. Moreover, a cohesive group should avoid backing a collection of individuals into too small a corner. We can never be sure who feels they have to defend what, and to whom. Thus, when planning a consciousness-raising activity with others, it's best to give your guests all the briefing you can. This is what his support group suggested to Chuck, the engineer trying to change his company's policy for improving manufacturing facilities. Before any meetings, he advised people which issues he wanted to discuss, and he tried not to present any surprises. He phrased discrepancies in terms that helped others see their own personal relationship to them, and kept in the background the conflicts he felt with their roles in producing discrepancies. He must have realized that it's all too easy for lower-level workers to state problems and ask questions, with the result that higher-level guests would feel they should have the solutions and answers to the problems posed.

On the other side, if we have upper-level status and we're trying to discuss discrepancies with lower-level managers, we must be sure to declare how the discrepancies we're discussing affect us, as well as our hunch that they create problems for our guests. For instance, if we want to open-endedly discuss working hours, we've got to be sure that they don't hear us saying that they should be more punctual. We need to emphasize that we want to benefit from what they've learned while coping with the discrepancy between posted working hours and the hours people have been keeping. When we hear lower-level guests merely anticipating what they think are our needs, then we've got to drop our agenda and turn to an explicit consideration of what should be done so that people can safely contribute their candid thoughts to the meeting. We must not assume that we can declare a truth session and have it, and we should not assume that people don't have valid reasons for objecting to one. If we succeed in overpowering their resistance to candor, we may unwittingly leave some people overexposed, and wind up with short-term gains at the expense of longer-term progress.

Reflection

Ultimately, we want organization members with various experiences to pool their perspectives and create a better, more complex picture of reality to guide the way the organization operates. I disagree with those who contend that this is happening to any extent today. What is happening is mainly people on the top channeling the rationales for their decisions downward. Now I don't need to be reminded that work has to be distributed within an organization; we all know it's inefficient for everyone to be involved in every decision. But only when people at every level have an opportunity to exchange relevant information can we build on the best of what each person has to offer. Together, we can create an organization system that helps us to express our potential.

CHAPTER 21

Conclusion:
The Importance
of Being Ourselves

Why would a Ph.D. chemist spend years trying to invent a new tooth-paste flavor? Why would an administrator spend his work life putting other people's plans into action? Why would a manager put in long hours away from home to earn money for stockholders he's never met? These people are not that different from us; in fact, they are us. Our commitment to the goals of the organizations for which we work exceeds the money we receive for our efforts. We are committed to our jobs because of the opportunities that they provide us with to do some-thing personally meaningful with our lives. We seek work that allows us to develop and expand our capabilities, and form associations that give a deep human dimension to our lives. Working to invent a new toothpaste flavor, to put the ideas of others into action, to earn money for stockholders are all vehicles for accomplishing something more important. Yet it's so easy to lose perspective and think these are our goals.

We have lived too long with the assumption that organizations are accountable only to their owners. They also should be accountable to us, the people who comprise organizations. We have staked our lives on their ability to provide us with meaningful and challenging work. We must not be unduly intimidated by the numbers of people who are worrying exclusively about rates of return on invested capital, per-formance effectiveness, or whatever, as if these constituted all there was to evaluating the organization's output. We can't afford to put our fates exclusively in the hands of people who don't relate to the greater meaning our work holds for us.

If we can't count on them, then we've got to count on ourselves! Each of us needs a personal frame of reference that gives focus and commitment to our projects and helps us see when our activities are out of sync with personal priorities. We know organization life is a compromise; we don't need to hear that one again. But we want to lead our lives with our compromises explicit. We want to know when we're in danger of sacrificing something that must not be compromised or when we're sacrificing more than we're receiving in exchange.

When we approach the organization with our own frame of reference, we run the risk of having such a narrow focus that all we get is what we expect. Creating an open-ended focus that still allows us to extract personal relevance from the infinitude of what's taking place depends on the types of questions we ask ourselves. When our questions are convergent, then our organization world becomes a closed system. But when our questions are phrased divergently, then we open ourselves to surprises, new meaning, and learning.

Asking the right kinds of questions, developing a frame of reference that allows us to be our own organization man, gets us to the point where we can declare ourselves and make our own special peace with the organization world, if only to revise it at another time. Making peace is not the same as copping out or retiring on the job. It means developing our own focus and pursuing it as long as it makes sense to us. During a candid discussion on career development, I heard a fifty-year-old manager with a solid record of organization service say to the big boss, "I don't want to be president. I don't even want to be a division head or an associate head. I'm no longer all that concerned with status. I don't have all the money that I could use, but I have all I need. I just want to be challenged." Then he turned down a promotion to manage a very large operation in a technical area in which he had years of experience, and volunteered to manage a small and little understood aspect of the company's business. It was an impressive moment.

But learning how to live with the divergent questions necessary for developing this kind of perspective is not all that easy. In the divergent thinking sessions I've led with management groups, I've never seen one go by without somebody becoming quite upset with the process. In a typical instance, a normally rational advertising manager stood up, red in the face, shouting, "I can't see where all this is going to get us," as if he was sure it was going to sweep us right down the tubes. And this was only ten minutes into an all-day meeting. A few minutes of gentle inquiry were all that was necessary to set him straight. It turned out that he wasn't even angry; he was anxious. Because he couldn't identify anything that could be making him anxious, he assumed he was angry, and seized upon a reason to explode. He had the right event, just the wrong emotion. In focusing divergently, we were violating a thought structure from which he normally derived security. As this became explicit, others admitted to their own uneasiness, and normal color returned to his face. The advertising manager then settled back and became a keen contributor.

Meeting organization life with a divergent focus requires support. Throughout this book I've emphasized the role a support group plays in helping us do this. Everyone I've ever seen make substantial progress has had the support of a group. People who lack understanding of how to get group support, or who exercise extreme discipline and aren't able to blow their cool, like the advertising manager blew his, do not get the support they need to aggressively seek out greater consciousness.

Perhaps the biggest obstacle to making organization life more consistent with our needs and interests lies in the difficulty people have in being themselves and holding candid discussions about the human elements in their work life. Even so-called human development experts are reluctant to approach human concerns directly. We have learned that it's easier to get an audience when we begin talking about new ways to improve productivity or increase work group effectiveness. We've taken this tack as a foot-in-the-door to getting people to talk about the personal and social qualities of their life in the organization. We reason that planners cannot think too long about productivity goals without thinking about the people involved. We reason that work groups can't talk too long about decision making and communications without discussing personal and interpersonal needs. But while our reasoning is logical enough, we often lose out in practice. We consistently underestimate the resistance people marshal when it comes time to exhibit and talk about the human and personal issues of their organization life. Too often our tactics wind up merely supporting the status quo!

Thus, I have my doubts about any strategy for organization change that indirectly approaches the human elements of organization life. I also have my doubts about any strategy that allows people at the top to plan for people on the bottom, or any strategy that features people at any level critiquing others, but not themselves.

More than anything else, I believe the quality of our organization life depends on the level of humanity and naturalness we're personally willing to discover and exhibit. We can't reasonably expect to exhibit more candor to others than we are willing to accept in ourselves. Self-candor begins with self-acceptance. We need to accept who we discover ourselves to be, and open-endedly inquire whether or not there's more. No doubt we'll uncover some crucial gaps between our ideals and our reality. Acknowledging these gaps and divergently reflecting on their meaning take us to the next frontier of self-understanding and expression.

0

Index